Love and PAIN
A SURVIVAL HANDBOOK FOR WOMEN

Sandra Horley grew up in Sarnia, Ontario, in Canada. She worked as a secretary in Montreal and then received a scholarship to study sociology at McGill University. She has also studied at the universities of Oxford and Birmingham.

Her first job in the field of woman abuse was as organiser of the Haven project in Wolverhampton. Since 1983 she has been director of Chiswick Family Rescue. She has also worked as a counsellor for abused women, as a homelessness officer in Shrewsbury, and as a housing advice worker in Brixton.

A committed campaigner on behalf of battered women, she gave evidence to the Metropolitan Police Working Party on Domestic Violence in 1985. She currently trains police, health, housing and social workers, and gives frequent talks and broadcasts.

Love and Pain is Sandra Horley's first book. She lives in North London with her photographer husband, Julian Nieman, and their daughter Samantha.

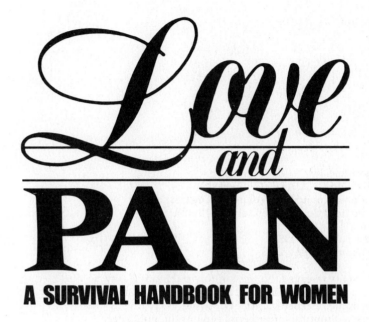

Love and PAIN

A SURVIVAL HANDBOOK FOR WOMEN

SANDRA HORLEY

Bedford Square Press

Published by
BEDFORD SQUARE PRESS of the
National Council for Voluntary Organisations
26 Bedford Square, London WC1B 3HU

First published 1988
© Sandra Horley 1988

ISBN 0 7199 1214 8

Typeset by Acorn Bookwork, Salisbury, Wilts
Printed and bound in England by Biddles, Guildford

The author and publisher have made every effort to ensure
that the information in this book was correct at the time of
going to press, but they cannot be held responsible for any
errors or changes in legislation.

A CIP catalogue record for this book is available from the
British Library.

Contents

Preface

I have written this book in the hope that it will break through the isolation and pain experienced by all abused women, whatever their circumstances, and help them to change their lives.

As an abused woman, you may not realise that what you are going through is termed 'abuse'. You may not realise that what starts as a slap or shove may lead to violent and regular beatings, and sometimes murder. You may find it easier to explain your partner's behaviour away by saying that he is overworked, under stress or has had too much to drink. But in the long run, in order to regain control over your life it will be necessary for you to face the reality of your situation. You cannot change your partner's behaviour but you can stop putting up with it.

This book is based on my experiences as a counsellor and as Director of Chiswick Family Rescue. In my work, I have listened to countless stories of abuse experienced by many women. Because of what these women have told me, I feel that there is a need, in a book of this kind, not only to offer practical advice, but also to reassure women that they are not responsible for their partner's abusive behaviour and that they do not have to put up with it. In this book I have quoted from women's descriptions of their experiences but for reasons of safety and privacy their names have been changed. In addition, I have quoted from women I have talked to informally – in buses, shops and streets – as well as those who, having discovered my job, began, for the first time, to talk about the abuse they have suffered.

Ten years ago, when I first started working with abused women, my own information about the subject was very limited. I was shocked, not only by the widespread extent of the problem in terms of physical violence, but also by the even more common emotional abuse. I have now counselled more than 2,000 abused women, and over and over again I hear horrifying stories of mental bullying and cruelty. Many women have told me that sometimes the emotional abuse is even worse than physical assault. Such cruelty can be devastating. If it goes on over a period of time it can make women feel worthless and trapped. It can lead to nervous breakdowns and even suicide.

I firmly believe that woman abuse – physical, emotional and sexual – is a problem facing society as a whole, not only the women who have to suffer it. Until men stop believing that they have the right to control women, they will continue to abuse women. As a society we must overcome our embarrassment and stop turning a blind eye to this injustice. We must step up pressure on the police to enforce the criminal law to protect women and their children. We must offer sympathetic help and support to all those involved. Most important, we must stop blaming women for the abuse. However, until society's attitudes have changed, woman abuse will remain a major problem to be tackled, and many thousands of women each year will need help.

There are a variety of approaches to dealing with woman abuse, because every woman, and every relationship, is unique. For example, some women will feel that they need the support of a refuge or women's group, or the help of their family and friends, before they are able to face up to, and acknowledge, the abuse they have suffered. Some women may prefer to seek help by themselves, and may feel that they simply want to follow some of the suggestions for positive action given in this book. There is no one method, no right or wrong way, of handling the problem. The important thing is to recognise that abuse is taking place and that it is possible, however helpless you feel, to stop abuse from ruling your life.

So what can you do if you are being subjected to physical or mental violence by the man with whom you are living? If you confide in your friends or neighbours, what can they do? If you go to a solicitor, how will you be able to afford their fees? Who can you turn to if your family urges you to stay with your husband to 'make a go' of your marriage? Where can you go if your friends won't believe you, or take your partner's side? How do you know your next relationship will be any better? This book will give you some answers to these questions, and help you take positive action to improve your life.

Written specifically for abused women and all the people who care for them, it gives straightforward, practical advice which will help women to recognise the danger signs and take preventative measures to ensure their own safety and emotional well-being. It will enable women who are physically, emotionally or sexually abused by their partners to make decisions with confidence and regain control over their lives. Women who think that their destiny is to suffer in lonely silence will discover that solutions to their problems do exist.

Sandra Horley

Acknowledgements

My grateful thanks to all those who made this book possible: the many courageous women who shared their stories with me; all at Chiswick Family Rescue and the Haven Project; Deborah Sinclair, David Currie, Lenore Walker and Bev Lever whose work helped crystallise my own ideas; in particular Fred Mashaal for his long-term and continued encouragement; Evelyn Kolish, Robert Dufresne, Dr D.J. McClure, Nancy, Harold and Annabelle Ship whose insights and support have enriched this book; Neville Vincent; Pete and Karen Townshend; Doreen Grinham; Ruby Brooke; Colin Brown; Libba Davies, whose brainstorms generated ideas for the book; Liz Collard, at the London Housing Centre, Sally Campbell at the Northern Ireland Association of Citizens Advice Bureaux; Alison Ball, barrister; David Nichols, solicitor; Alison Strode, whose writing talent and humour saved the day on more than one occasion; Mary Finn, for her comments on the manuscript; Carol Smith, my agent; Jacqueline Sallon, editor of the Bedford Square Press, for her expert advice and guidance; Shirley Jane Horley, my mother, for her steadfastness and love from over the seas; Aileen Nieman for being such a wonderful grandmother to Samantha during a particularly busy period of our lives; and most of all to Julian Nieman, my husband, whose support and faith were crucial: in addition to his warmth, love and patience, he gave endless hours to help this book become a reality; and finally, to 'Sam', our daughter, whose energy and joy are a constant source of inspiration.

1 Introduction

What is woman abuse?

Woman abuse involves the repeated, habitual and random use of intimidation, whether by physical or verbal aggression, to force a woman to submit to her partner's demands. If a woman is forced to alter her behaviour because she is frightened of her partner's reaction, then their relationship is abusive.

Although there is so much abuse of women in the home, recognising the fact is not always straightforward. If all you look for is the stereotype of a woman with a black eye and an 18-stone, drunken husband, then you will fail to notice many instances of abuse.

Abuse can occur without breaking bones or visible signs of bruising. Often abuse is emotional and psychological – for example ridicule, ill-treating children and hurting family pets can be attempts by a man to control his partner's behaviour, that is, to abuse her.

Woman abuse is rarely discussed. It happens in secret and, because the woman usually lives with the man who assaults her, it is very seldom that anyone outside the home knows that the abuse is taking place. Most people do not seem to realise that countless women are being deprived of their basic human rights. Nor do they understand that physically assaulting a woman in the home, like mugging or any other form of assault, is against the law. If the assault happened in public there would be outrage. Because it happens behind closed doors ('An Englishman's home is his castle') people feel they should not interfere. People are also shocked by wife abuse. They feel it is 'unnatural', and they do not like to admit it happens. Therefore the whole subject becomes taboo. When it is discussed, women are blamed for the abuse. Statements such as 'she must have deserved it' or 'she provoked it' are commonplace. It is somehow easier for society to assume that women are responsible for violence against them than to acknowledge that men are perpetrating abuse.

Extent of the problem

According to 1986 statistics, in the metropolitan area of London alone about 28,000 calls were made to the police concerning physical assaults against women in the home. Researchers estimate that in fact the number of incidents is nearer three to four times this amount. As well as the reported physical violence, there is widespread emotional abuse.

The following figures give some indication of the extent of the problem:

- One in four women has been hit by her partner.[1]
- In 10 per cent of all murders in London, a wife, or common-law wife, is the victim of her husband or male partner.[2]
- One study into the police response to domestic violence indicated that over 1,000 women a week in London contact the Metropolitan Police for help.[3]
- A Canadian study showed that women (on average) are beaten 35 times before they contact the police for help.[4]
- The findings from one British study suggest that over half a million women who have been assaulted by their partners seek police help in Britain each year.[5]

(For detailed references to these findings, please see page 105.)

It is a mistake to think that woman abuse is merely a freak occurrence. The opposite is true. It is as widespread as the common cold, but it has far more damaging effects on its victims – affecting their personalities and their ability to play an active part in society.

Part 1

Recognising the Problem

2 Physical abuse

Physical abuse is usually the most recognisable form of abuse. Attacks can result in black eyes, cut lips, fractured skulls and bruising. Sometimes they are even more vicious. For example, take the cases of the woman whose husband mutilated her face with a hammer and chisel or the woman whose husband broke her arm in three places as she breast-fed their newborn baby. Physical abuse can also cause miscarriages, blindness, deafness and other permanent injuries.

Perhaps you think you are not a 'battered woman' because you have not suffered such extreme violence. You may just have been slapped or shoved occasionally by your partner. Or he may have pulled your hair or just waved his fist in your face. Perhaps he has spat on you or restrained you unecessarily during a row. These assaults may seem slight compared with the horror tales one sometimes hears, but such behaviour is dangerous and can become more serious over time.

Unfortunately, some women do not see that they are victims of physical assault. Mary said: 'My husband isn't violent really; the most he has done is smash eggs over my head.' Cynthia said that her partner only pushed her once in a while, or that he slapped her across the face from time to time, but 'nothing more serious than that'. These incidents, whether they occurred in public or in private, are typical examples of physical abuse. Although no physical scars were left in either case, the humiliation inflicted physically can only be termed as abuse, and it is unacceptable. What may start as a slap or a shove can become a repeated pattern of violent and regular beatings and, in some cases, can terminate in murder.

Although it may be tempting to dismiss a first slap as a harmless outburst of frustration, do not underestimate the seriousness of any attack by your partner (whether it is an actual assault or the threat of assault). Once the abuse starts it can get progressively more severe. Abused women often report that violence can erupt quite unexpectedly after years of being together. Elaine makes this point:

For the first 10, 11 years, he was quite mild. Then, out of the blue, he began saying to me, 'You've not had a good hiding lately, have you?' He would try to wind me up so that I would say something that wasn't right. Then he would have a reason to hit me. This went on for about a year. I am not saying there weren't any good times, because there were, but I never knew when to expect the abuse. It didn't happen very often, but after the first episode he seemed to think it was his right.

People often assume that a pregnancy will bring harmony to the family and protect the woman. However, many abused women have told of violence during pregnancy. The reason may be that some men feel that a child will threaten their possession of the mother. Not only is a pregnant woman in this situation less able to defend herself, her unborn child is also at risk. As Nagul described:

The first time he hit me was when I was pregnant. Over the months he got more and more aggressive. Everything I did was wrong. When I was 8 months pregnant he completely lost control and kicked me in the stomach. I was covered in bruises but no one in the family seemed to take any notice. In Sri Lanka beating your wife is as common as sneezing. I was afraid that the baby wouldn't live. She came before her time, but luckily it didn't harm her.

Another woman told how the problems in her marriage started when she became pregnant:

It was five years before I fell pregnant with Julie. We were fairly happy until then, but when she was born he didn't bother to come to see us in hospital. That broke my heart. It was hard. It was a mental thing he was doing to me. He used to hit me when I was carrying her, but not coming to hospital was more painful really. I couldn't understand what I had done to make him behave like this.

Physical abuse also leaves emotional scars. It can make the strongest woman feel humiliated, ashamed and embarrassed. It undermines self-confidence and chips away at self-respect. Over time it can stop you from going about your daily routine. You may become so paralysed with feelings of powerlessness and hopelessness that you find it difficult to make minor decisions. As Carolyn explained:

I never knew what was going to set him off. Living with him, I was so wound up I couldn't make up my mind what to buy at the shops — even things that had nothing to do with him like my tampons or my shampoo. I would just be too anxious to make the choice.

You may become so apathetic that you reluctantly accept abuse from your partner. Maybe you feel that there is nothing you can do to improve the situation so you give up trying. As Diane explained:

Some mornings I just didn't feel like getting out of bed. I wanted to die. However much I tried to be positive I still felt overwhelmed by it all.

Many abused women feel weak and helpless, although, in reality, they have an enormous amount of strength. The problem is that their strength is being used up surviving from day to day.

Abused women frequently tell me that they wish their husbands would leave them or find someone else. In some cases they fantasise about killing them to stop the abuse. Whatever happens in your relationship, physical abuse is unacceptable. Your partner may say you provoked him, but no 'provocation' can justify violent behaviour. Assault is against the law and you do not have to put up with it.

3 Sexual abuse

The sexual act can be an expression of love, giving pleasure equally to both participants. In abusive relationships the sexual act can be an expression of violence. Some men use sex in order to control a woman's behaviour as well as to assert their authority and dominance in the relationship. Sex is sometimes used as a punishment.

Sexual abuse can range from mildly offensive behaviour to total humiliation and physical danger. A common form of sexual abuse is when a man insists on having sex regardless of his partner's feelings. Gail said:

He expected sex every night, no matter how tired I was. I realised very early on in our relationship that it was easier to go along with him than refuse.

Sexual abuse can also include a man ogling other women in front of his partner, thereby damaging her self-esteem and sexual identity; preventing her from using birth control by taking away or destroying contraceptives; demanding sex whenever the whim takes him; criticising her performance in bed; forcing her to have anal sex and to participate in other sexual activities which she may find disgusting; pushing objects into her vagina or anus; intimidating her into having sex with other men while he looks on; forcing her to have intercourse in front of the children; physically injuring a woman during sex or threatening her with violence if she refuses.

Judy described how sex with her partner became humiliating and disgusting:

He was like an animal in bed. Sometimes he would play with himself when I was asleep and then come all over my face. In the beginning he made me have sex every night and sometimes he would wake me up in the night expecting it. I wasn't allowed to say no. I was a virgin when I married him. I just assumed it was all part of marriage. I woke up one morning and he was trying to shove something up me. I got angry but he gave me a backhander in the face. In the end I even hated sleeping in the same bed. I didn't want him to touch me.

Often abusive men tell their partners that they are lesbians or that they are frigid. Marilyn said of her marriage.

When I think now, I was raped quite a few times. He used to say 'You're frigid, you are useless in bed. I don't know why I married you.' Now for years and years and years, I thought that was my fault.

These men fail to realise that it is their own behaviour that has made their partners withdraw emotionally and physically. Showing love for someone is difficult if you are afraid of how that person sometimes abuses you. It is understandable that the more fearful a woman is the less likely she will feel able to enjoy sex with her partner.

Abusers sometimes feel that they are entitled to have sexual intercourse whenever they desire it. However, even a marriage licence does not entitle a man to use his wife's body in any way that gives him pleasure. Forcing sexual intercourse on a woman without consent is *rape* and has devastating consequences (although rape in marriage is not yet recognised by the law in Britain).

One abused woman told how her husband had brutally raped her three days after the birth of their child, causing her stitches to burst open. Afterwards, he could not understand what all the fuss was about. Another woman described the very real fear she felt when her ex-boyfriend had forced her to have sex at knifepoint. The emotional trauma of sexual abuse is illustrated in the case of a woman who attempted suicide after her husband forced her to have anal sex in front of her children.

There are two commonly-held myths about sexual abuse:

Myth No. 1 Sexual violence is an extra-strong expression of love by someone with a healthy sexual appetite. *Not true. A man who forces sex on a woman is not expressing love for her; what he is in love with is his power over her. A man does not have rights of ownership over a woman's body.*

Myth No. 2 A woman who resists sexual approaches wants to be dominated sexually. *Not true. Many women feel powerless and submit only because of their real fear and terror. Forcing a woman to have sexual intercourse is not only degrading and humiliating, it can cause permanent physical injury and severe emotional trauma. Sexual abuse is not merely a disagreement about how a couple should enjoy sex together. It is a sexual relationship which has gone seriously wrong.*

If you feel disgusted, humiliated or degraded when having sexual relations with your partner, you are being abused. No one should be forced to participate in sexual acts which they find unpleasant. You have the right to choose when to have sexual relations. You have rights over your own body.

4 Emotional abuse

Emotional abuse is an attack on a woman's personality rather than on her body. Like physical abuse, it is used by the man to undermine and control his partner. The weapons of emotional abuse include threats of violence, humiliation, verbal and psychological harassment, lies and manipulation, blackmail, withholding money and isolating the woman from family and friends.

Frequently, battered women report that emotional abuse can be as crippling as physical assault. One woman living in a refuge had her jaw broken in five places and still maintained that the emotional abuse had been far worse than the physical violence. Unfortunately, many women do not recognise that they are victims of emotional or psychological abuse. It can be used to sap a woman's will to do anything other than what she is told to do. As one woman said:

It is a bit like torture. When somebody has treated you very badly and then comforts you, you feel so alone and so grateful to receive that comfort and so glad you are not being abused, that you accept it. I suppose like all prisoners who have been tortured, you start to feel a certain amount of sympathy for your torturer. Also, during the good times I lost my ability to remember the abuse. It was as if I had fantasised it, as if I had made it up.

When you are suffering emotional abuse it is easy for the reality of your situation to become distorted. The longer you are abused the more you believe your partner's insults. His persistence and your dependency on him make you more vulnerable to his criticisms. You doubt yourself and stop trusting your feelings. You begin to deny that the abuse is taking place or minimise the effect of it. Denying abuse seems easier than facing up to it. Facing up to it seems so hard because it involves taking responsibility for changing your situation. Denial protects you from feeling the pain that comes from knowing that the person you think you love and trust is not lovable and dependable. This knowledge causes you to experience conflicting emotions such as fear, anger, shame, resentment, sadness and helplessness. To avoid the pain these feelings cause, you blame yourself for the abuse, or else deny it is taking place. Or you may choose to ignore it and hope that it won't ever happen again. You want the abuse to go away, but you shy away from the responsibility of doing something about it.

How to recognise emotional abuse

The following examples will help you to recognise emotional abuse. Does your partner say:

- You're crazy, I will have you committed to a mental hospital.
- You're hysterical. No one will believe you.
- You couldn't possibly manage without me. You'd never cope on your own.
- Nobody else would have you. You can't cope with a real relationship.
- You are a slag/whore/bitch/tart/slut.
- You look awful. You've got a terrible body.
- You're mad/you're loony.
- Leave if you want to but how do you think you will live? I'm telling you – you and the bloody kids will be on the street.
- You won't get a thing out of social security. I've got the order books.
- If you divorce me you won't get custody of the children. I'll tell social services you are a drug addict/alcoholic/liar/unfit mother.
- If you leave me my career will be ruined and it'll be all your fault.
- If you divorce me I will make sure you don't get a penny from the courts.
- If you leave me I shall kill myself.
- If you try to escape I shall kill you and the children.
- If you try anything I'll have you deported.
- You leave, and I'll come after you and beat your brains out.
- I'll tell your friends/family/boss what a bad wife you are.

- If you leave I'll kidnap the children and take them abroad.

  If your partner says any of these things to you, then you are being emotionally abused.

Other signs of emotional abuse

If your partner does any of the following, you are being emotionally abused:

- threatens you, or others close to you, with violence
- gives away or kills the family pet
- smashes up the furniture or destroys your personal possessions
- humiliates you in front of others
- ridicules you when the children are around
- forces you to do degrading things such as kneeling down to beg forgiveness
- constantly lies to you
- unjustly accuses you of having affairs with other men
- insults you publicly or privately
- says you are cold/frigid/a lesbian
- frightens you by waving weapons in front of you when he is angry
- discourages you from having friends or seeing your family
- bullies you, harasses you and sometimes argues late into the night merely to win a point
- behaves like a dictator, ruling your every action (for example, by telling you what to wear, when to brush your teeth, how to behave)
- refuses to give you money, then complains that there isn't enough food
- forbids you to use the family car, if you have one, in order to isolate you
- withholds affection to punish you
- locks you out of the house during a row
- constantly criticises everything you do
- has sudden changes of mood which dominate the household
- over-reacts to minor irritations and does not control his rages

If he does any of the above, he is using emotional abuse to control you.

5 Who are the offenders?

There are many misunderstandings about the kinds of men who abuse their partners. Rather than examine the facts, many people choose to say woman abuse is caused by stress, unemployment, alcoholism or mental illness or else to describe it as occurring only among certain groups in society, for example, the working classes. In fact, men who batter their partners come from all walks of life, all cultures and all religions. Wives of vicars, doctors and lawyers are as much at risk as women living with unskilled workers.

It is sometimes said that alcohol *causes* wife abuse. Although some abusers may have problems with alcohol or drugs, this is often used as an *excuse* to be violent. In many cases a man with a drink problem still abuses his partner when he is not drinking. Assaults are committed by sober men too. Blaming alcohol or drugs is a way of avoiding taking responsibility for the problem.

Batterers are generally not insane or mentally ill. Research shows that the proportion of mentally ill people among batterers is no higher than in the population as a whole. Men who batter are usually controlled enough not to hit their employers or people on the street, but they feel no need to use self-control at home, where they hit their partners.

Abusers can appear to be perfectly normal, charming people in every aspect of their lives – except when they are alone with their families. Often it is hard for outsiders to imagine that abusers are capable of hurting anyone. Far too often a woman's story of abuse is not believed. There are various reasons for this: a husband may well deny what is happening in order to protect himself; often an abuser presents a different side of his personality to people outside the home. When a woman is involved in an abusive relationship with a man who has a clearly-defined status within the community (such as a doctor, lawyer, dentist, schoolteacher or Member of Parliament), it is even less likely that her stories will be believed. In fact, because of her partner's position it is unlikely that she will confide in anyone, since to do so would damage his reputation and professional status.

In those professions where status is defined by rank, such as the armed services and the police force, men are trained to use violence when necessary either in self-defence or in warfare. These men have unquestioned authority at work and sometimes expect the same kind of obedience at home. This is no excuse for the use of violence in the home. The following description is typical of such a relationship:

He ruled the house with a rod of iron. He made all the decisions, like who was allowed to visit, what we would watch on television. He always wanted me to be home before he got in. The children had to go to bed by 6.30, otherwise he would fly into an uncontrollable rage. I used to work all day and wanted to spend time with them in the evenings but he always insisted that 6:30 was bedtime. Sometimes I used to sneak upstairs to talk to them and give them a quick cuddle. If he caught me he would shout and argue for hours. It was as if he was jealous of his own children. Whatever it was he had to have the final say. His word was law.

Some women who have been involved in abusive relationships over a period of years report that their partners showed no sign of violence before the marriage (or co-habitation), while others say that looking back they realised that there were warning signs. Obviously these warning signs vary in every relationship, but there are certain recurring patterns which may become apparent before a relationship becomes permanent.

Warning signs

- Is your partner possessive? Does he object if you make plans that don't include him?
- Is he dominating? Does he choose what you wear, criticise your clothes, make-up or your behaviour in public?
- Does he have firm ideas about what men should do and what women should be? Does he believe that men should have the final say in the household? Often this kind of man feels entitled to control his partner.
- Is he jealous? If you talk to other men does he accuse you of being unfaithful? Is he jealous of your relationships with women friends and family?

- Does he make excessive demands on your time? Does he constantly check what you are doing, or telephone you at work or at home, sometimes for trivial reasons? Abusers often feel the need to check up on their partners, because they are jealous of them.
- Does he make all the decisions in the relationship (who to see, where to go, what to eat, how to spend the housekeeping money)?
- Does he lose his temper over trivial matters? Often a potential abuser will then over-compensate with presents of flowers, perfume or chocolates.
- Does he give others the impression of being a 'really nice man' and then behave differently when you are alone?
- What were his own family relationships like? Was he himself physically abused? Often a man who was physically abused by his father or who witnessed physical abuse of his mother becomes abusive in adult relationships.[6] (However not all the children who have been the victims of physical abuse become batterers as adults).[7]
  (See page 105 for full references to these findings.)
- Does he seem to feel inadequate in any way at all? Does he complain incessantly or unreasonably about his workmates, or blame other people for his problems?
- Does he shout or hit you and then blame you for what happened (saying 'you provoked me', 'you made me do it')? Does he seek to explain away, or try to forget his behaviour?

If the answer to any of these questions is 'yes', then your partner could have abusive tendencies.

Can a batterer be reformed?

A common mistake that many women make is to imagine that marriage will change their partner, and, like the prince and the princess in the fairy story, they will all live happily ever after. In the case of wife abusers, this is simply not true. These men seem to believe that a marriage licence or a shared front door key gives them rights of ownership over their partner's body and soul. Although North American studies suggest that it is possible for batterers to learn new attitudes and new behaviour, such a change is, unfortunately, very rare. Most abusers deny that there is a problem at all, or they convince themselves that it is not serious. This prevents them from taking the first step in changing their behaviour. Some batterers do seek professional help from social workers or marriage guidance counsellors. But all too often, they say that they are expecting to stop the abuse by persuading their wives to change, or by adjusting imaginary 'wrongs' in the relationship. More often than not these abusers have difficulty in accepting that is is *they* who must do the changing.

If you are an abused woman it is important to understand that your partner's abuse can only stop if he accepts responsibility for his behaviour and has a genuine desire to change himself. As long as he goes on blaming you, or your relationship, for his actions, his abusive behaviour will continue.

6 Effects of abuse

If you have been subjected to physical, sexual or emotional abuse you will undoubtedly experience negative feelings: worthlessness, shame, degradation, helplessness, humiliation, fear and/or guilt. The consequence of these feelings can be a profound loss of self-respect and feelings of personal worth. It is helpful to understand how this pattern develops.

In a healthy relationship the games between partners are affectionate and playful – for example, using childish nicknames. In an abusive relationship these games can be used to lower a woman's opinion of herself and eventually even to humiliate and frighten her. If a woman is living in a threatening situation it is easy for an abusive partner to intimidate her by suddenly slamming a door, by abruptly turning the television off or on, or by altering the volume on the radio. Often the abuser takes an almost sadistic pleasure in frightening his victim before any verbal or physical confrontation takes place. Beverly describes how she felt:

The tension was unbearable at times. I felt so nervous and jumpy. I never knew when he was going to lose his temper. He shouted all the time. Once he chased me with a hammer. I thought he was going to kill me. He made me take off my wedding ring and then hammered it until it was completely flat.

Another way of gradually wearing down the woman's spirit is by continually nagging. Sometimes events from 18 months back are singled out for criticism although these details may have been discussed many times before. As Charlene explains:

Every time we had an argument I knew he would go back to that time I danced with his brother at the wedding. He would start shouting 'you filthy, black whore, you oughta show me more respect'. This went on forever. No matter how hard I tried telling him it's only a dance, isn't it, he went on accusing me, telling me I had it off with his brother . . . It was so bleeding stupid . . . he used to wear me out. I can hear him now, going on and on about this dumb dance.

Such 'discussions' can last until the small hours of the morning or until the woman's patience snaps; she may shout or even hit back and this can result in physical assault from her partner. She may feel guilty about the incident, believing she has provoked the assault by shouting. The abuser may well make a big show of 'forgiving' his partner for her provocative behaviour, reinforcing her belief that she is to blame.

A 68-year-old widow suffered 40 years of misery until her husband died. Enid recalls:

*One Sunday I spent all morning cooking a special dinner for Jim. He said he would just nip down to the local for a quick pint. I done him a lovely roast, with all the trimmings, Yorkshire pud . . . the lot. I laid the table and waited and waited. By the time he got in the dinner was ruined. I was really upset after all that effort. He took one look at it and said 'You don't expect me to eat that *** rubbish do you? I'm starving. Cook me something decent.' That was more than I could take. All these years I'd kept quiet but this time I flipped my lid. I grabbed the dishes and chucked the dinner at his feet. Then he went for me, hammer and tongs. I was so terrified this time he would kill me, so I begged for mercy. He made me kneel down on the floor like he was God or something. Then made a big do about forgiving me and all that. He didn't think for a second that he was to blame.*

Sometimes merely the sound of her partner's key in the front door can so alarm the abused woman that she becomes jittery and this irritates him. In turn, his irritation makes her more nervous and it is easy to persuade her that she is indeed 'crazy', 'mad' or 'stupid'.

The longer you live in an atmosphere of mistrust and terror the worse you will feel. You may have tried, unsuccessfully, to stop your partner from abusing you. Each defeat lowers your self-respect. Your enforced isolation makes you more dependent on your partner. You stop trusting your feelings or believing in your own judgement. Gradually you may come to the conclusion that you are to blame for what is happening to you. You begin to accept your partner's criticisms and believe him when he says that the abuse is your fault. But whatever changes you make he continues to abuse you. With time you start to feel that you have no control over your life. The abuse gradually wears away your self-respect and damages your spirit. It fosters feelings of inadequacy, despair and disillusionment. You become resigned and give up trying to control your life. Philomena describes the effects of abuse:

We were so in love at first, it's hard to believe he's the same man. I can't understand why he behaves the way he does. I don't just mean the violence . . . that doesn't happen very often, but the verbal abuse and the bullying. He can be so crazy at times, like the time he held a pillow over my face. I nearly suffocated. He threw me out of the house once, in the middle of the night. I was 8 months pregnant and it was raining, but I was too afraid and too ashamed to go for help. A few months ago he poured petrol over me and the children and made us sit there, told us he'd set us on fire if we moved. He forgets how he behaves. This sort of thing happens and afterwards he'll act as if everything is OK. It seems like every time I let down my guard he starts bullying me and telling me I am pathetic, that I'm no good, that he doesn't know why he married me. I am anxious all the time, living in constant fear. I am afraid I'll say the wrong thing, cook something he doesn't like . . . I'm living on the edge all the time. When he is good, he is really good. It doesn't make sense. He can be so kind and then suddenly he goes all out of control. I think he loves me really, but why does he hurt me? I try hard to please him, I can't be all that bad. But then maybe I am to blame . . . I don't know anymore. I don't know what's real and what isn't.

Prolonged abuse can cause physical illnesses. Many abused women suffer from ailments such as heart failure, ulcers, migraine, insomnia, stomach upsets and high blood pressure. Sometimes depression or an anxiety state is diagnosed by a doctor and tranquillizers are prescribed. Some women become dependent on tablets or alcohol to help them cope. These can undermine you by making you think you are sick or unbalanced, when your depression is entirely justified, given your circumstances.

Over time, the inevitable consequence of such abuse is that you become convinced of your own worthlessness. You may start to believe that you are responsible for all the problems in your relationship. It can therefore be very difficult for you to recognise that you are, in fact, being abused. How then can you begin to realise the truth of your situation?

7 Are you an abused woman?

If your partner has abused you, you may have become lonely and isolated. For various reasons you may feel that you have no friends, and no one to whom you can turn for support. If your partner has convinced you that you are either mad or stupid, you may believe that other people think so too. Try to remember that this is not the case. You alone know all the details of the relationship with your partner. Only you know what happens behind your closed front door.

However isolated or depressed you feel, there will be moments when you also feel angry and resentful. These feelings are a healthy sign that you have recognised that you are being treated badly. Don't feel ashamed of them or try to bottle them up. If you suppress your anger it can work against you (for example, by making you feel depressed or by causing you to lose patience with your children). Conversely, once you admit that you feel anger, then it can be used positively to give you extra strength for making changes. Anger and resentment are signs that you recognise your rights as an individual.

Follow your instincts. Recognise your feelings. Remember that no one has the right to victimise another person. The problem won't go away until you admit to yourself that you are being abused and channel your anger into positive action. You cannot stop your partner from being abusive, but you don't have to put up with it.

If you answer 'yes' to the following questions, the chances are that you are being abused:
- Are you afraid of your partner?
- Do you become over-anxious if you are not at home to receive your partner's telephone calls or greet him from work?

- Do you feel frightened to ask him for housekeeping money?
- Are you entirely dependent on your partner?
- Are you isolated? Have you lost contact with your parents, family and friends?
- Do you assume that your partner is entitled to make all the rules and decisions in the home?
- Do you suffer from stress-related complaints such as headaches, insomnia and stomach problems? Are you anxious and depressed?
- Do you use alcohol or drugs excessively?
- Do you tell lies or deceive people in order to avoid making your partner angry?
- Does your behaviour change when your partner is present – from being friendly and sociable to being shy and inhibited?
- Have you ever attempted suicide?
- Are you anxious to avoid making your partner angry? Do you always accept his views and attitudes in order to keep the peace?
- Are you often kept awake late into the night by your partner arguing, often over something trivial or over past conflicts?
- Do you ignore your own needs (and sometimes your children's) in favour of his?
- Do you doubt your judgement and sometimes think you are going mad? Do you blame yourself for the problems in the relationship?

Part II

Facing up to the Problem

8 What you can do

Having realised – possibly for the first time – that you are being abused, what can you do? Recognising that you do not have to put up with abuse can be a first step. Taking more control of your life will be another. This does not necessarily mean making sudden changes or ending the relationship, but it will involve taking responsibility for the choices you make.

This may be particularly difficult if you have been abused. Up until now, your partner may have dominated your life and undermined your confidence. You may feel that you are on a treadmill of problems and that there are no solutions. It may seem easier just to do what you are told. However, in the long run, considering your options and making your own decisions will increase your self-respect and help you to take control of your own life.

Seeking advice from friends, social workers or marriage guidance counsellors can help you to identify your problems and make choices about how to solve them, but remember, in order to regain control of your life *you* will have to make the decisions. No one else will know what is the right solution for you.

Being in control also means making decisions at your own pace. You may need time to come to terms with your situation. Acting in accordance with your own wishes will boost your self-esteem and give you the confidence you need to move forward.

When you begin to face up to the problem of abuse you will probably feel conflicting emotions: anxiety, grief, guilt, shame, and hatred may all be mixed with love, anger, despair and hopelessness. Experiencing these emotions can be confusing. For example, you may feel it is best to leave your partner, but do not know where you will get the courage. You may want to talk to someone about the abuse, but are too ashamed. You may still love your partner but want him to stop abusing you. Although there are no instant solutions, there are steps you can take which will help.

1 Stop denying that there is a problem

As long as you deny that the abuse exists it will continue. You may find it hard to label yourself a 'battered woman', but you can't stop the abuse while you pretend that it is not taking place. Facing up to the problem may be scary, but it is easier, in the long run, than denying it. Dealing with the problem becomes progressively easier because each time you act and face reality you will prove to yourself that you are able to cope.

2 Stop taking the blame

In your confusion it may be easy for your partner or others to convince you that the abuse is your fault. Do not believe them. Your partner is responsible for his behaviour. You cannot make him abuse you against his will; the choice is his. Blaming yourself will enable your partner to continue denying that he has a problem. It is impossible for you to stop him being an abuser, but you can stop being his victim.

3 Get help

Reaching out for help is a brave and positive step. You may feel ashamed and embarrassed about revealing the abuse to others, but remember, it is not your fault. There are people who can and want to help you.

There are different kinds of help which you can look for. One is the personal support given by a friend, neighbour, workmate or relative who listens and believes your story. This support will help you to talk through your own ideas and feelings without being told what to do. A women's refuge or women's group will also provide emotional support. Working things out with other women in an atmosphere of self-help can be a very valuable way of breaking down your isolation and overcoming abuse. There are refuges in every part of the country (see pages 44–46 for more detailed information).

Another kind of help is available from voluntary agencies and professionals such as social workers, teachers, Samaritans, marriage guidance counsellors, Alcoholics Anonymous, law centres and citizens advice bureaux. They can advise you of your rights, offer information, discuss possible steps to take and, in some cases (for example, solicitors or the police), may take action on your behalf. The more information you have about the choices open to you, the easier it will be to regain control of your life. (For more information on agencies offering help and support see chapter 10 and appendix 1.)

Getting help is not an admission of defeat. It is a healthy move to make. You may have mixed feelings towards your partner and feel you are betraying him. You may think that telling someone about the problem will make matters worse. In fact, the reverse is true. Keeping it secret enables your partner to continue the abuse. Getting help does not necessarily mean ending your relationship, but it can enable you to see your situation more clearly. Living with abuse is stressful. It can make you feel powerless and unsure of yourself. Just talking to another person can help you to explore and understand your own feelings. You will probably find that you are not alone with this problem. Being with others who can understand your needs and your experiences will boost your self-confidence.

Whoever you turn to for help, two things are important: make sure that you choose someone who believes your story and that you are not pressurised into taking action against your will. If you feel that the advice you are getting is unsympathetic, do not be afraid to look elsewhere for help.

4   Break your isolation

Living in an abusive relationship may have made you feel isolated and dependent on your partner. Instinctively you may feel that your partner's behaviour is unreasonable, but the more isolated you become the harder it is to trust your own judgement. Gradually the abuse wears down your self-esteem, which makes it easier for your partner to convince you that you are worthless.

It is therefore important to re-establish contact with the world beyond your home. Taking part in outside activities will give you a new view of yourself to compare with your partner's view. You may discover that you are not as dependent on him as you thought. If you have been particularly isolated, changing your situation may simply mean talking to your mother, visiting a neighbour or renewing contact with an old friend.

You might consider enrolling in a class, joining a local volunteer group or looking for a job. It is unreasonable for your partner to object. If he does, you could consider going ahead without his permission. You may find that once you have started an activity he will not object to your carrying on with it. This could be the first step out of your isolation. Although you have every right to have contacts outside the home, do not overlook your safety. An abusive partner may feel threatened by your increased independence and become more aggressive. Break your isolation in ways which do not put you in danger. Only you can judge how far you can assert yourself and still keep safe.

Your new friends or your renewed acquaintances may not, however, be the people you want to entrust with your problems. If so, remember that you can keep them to yourself. It is not necessary to avoid contact with other people just because you wish to keep your private life to yourself.

5 Stop being so hard on yourself

Abuse creates feelings of guilt, worthlessness and helplessness. Often an abused woman forgets who she is or that she has any value as a person. Your partner may reinforce these feelings by continually pointing out your mistakes and shortcomings, but there is no need for you to dwell on them too. Instead, learn to think about yourself in a positive way. You can start by recognising your capabilities, like being able to care for your children or hold down a job under such difficult circumstances. Praise yourself for your successes and accomplishments, however small. Give yourself credit for getting through each day. You have, after all, shown considerable strength and courage by coping with the abuse up until now. You can use this strength to help develop a positive attitude about yourself. The more positive you feel the more likely it is that you will find a satisfactory solution to your problems.

6 Build your self-esteem

Many women who are no longer abused look back and see that their situation began to change once they increased their self-esteem. Having self-esteem means that you believe you are an important, worthwhile person. You recognise that you don't have to be perfect, and that you don't have to compare yourself with other people. You accept and value who you are and don't need to pretend to be somebody else. Having self-esteem means you see yourself as likeable and deserving of respect. If your partner has been telling you how bad or crazy you are over a period of time you may have begun to believe him. Instead of valuing yourself you may have developed very negative feelings about yourself. You may feel worthless and helpless.

How do you recognise low self-esteem?

- Do you hear yourself saying:
  'I should have done . . .'
  'I ought to have said . . .'
  'If only I had . .'
- Do you constantly apologise?
- Are you indecisive? People with low self-esteem are indecisive because they do not trust their own judgement.
- Do you worry about what others will think of you?
- Are you confident when you are at work or with friends but at home find that events and feelings are out of your control?
- Do you say 'yes' when you would really rather say 'no'?
- Do you feel unlikeable?
- Do you wish you were someone else?

If you answer 'yes' to any of these questions you are undervaluing yourself. This can make you more vulnerable because you may suspect that abuse is all you deserve.

To increase your self-esteem you need to do something positive, however small. This could be meeting new people or doing things which bring you fulfilment. Taking risks such as getting a job, accepting an invitation or getting involved in a new activity will help you, whether you stay in the abusive relationship or not. Building self-esteem is a gradual process. Every positive step you take will strengthen your self-esteem and enable you to make changes.

7 Focus on your own needs

In a healthy relationship, each partner cares for the other's emotional needs. In an abusive relationship a woman is likely to sacrifice her needs and devote herself to the welfare of her partner, without being cared for in return. Her whole personality can disappear beneath the full-time job of keeping him from getting angry. Living with abuse may have worn you down and perhaps made you lose sight of your own emotional needs, even though they are vital to your self respect. And, as you revive your self-respect you will gain the strength to change your life. Perhaps you feel you just do not have the energy to do this. However, even the realisation that you have needs is a good start. Paying attention to these needs will help you even more.

You do not have to wait for your partner to change before doing this. Start by setting aside an hour a day for yourself. If this is impossible try at least taking five minutes to imagine what you would do with your hour. Take an exercise class or read a book, visit a friend, go for a walk or to the swimming baths. The main thing is that whatever you do should not involve looking after others, because their needs would stop you from finding out about yourself, and what your own needs really are.

8   Increase your independence

Frequently, abused women are not allowed to make any decisions in their relationships; this makes them more dependent on their partners. In fact, some women believe that decision-making is the man's role and that they have no choice but to be dependent. Even if you do believe your partner should make the decisions, he does not have the right to abuse you. If you are denied freedom in your relationship, or if your partner controls or dominates you, it may be hard to imagine that one day you could be free. You may not have the confidence that you need to be independent simply because you have not had enough experience of taking responsibility. Why not try learning a new skill, joining a local women's or community group? New ventures like these could help you discover that you are capable of acting without your partner. Overcoming your anxiety about doing things you haven't done before may seem hard at first. However, once you have begun your confidence will grow.

Learning to be more independent will help you regain control and make decisions about your life. Constructing a new lifestyle – if necessary – may not seem such a daunting prospect if you have already been practising your independence.

9 Plan for an emergency

An emergency can mean different things to different women. Living in physically abusive relationships means that you run the risk of being assaulted by your partner at any time. If you are emotionally abused, an emergency might occur during a verbal attack by your partner. Whatever form the abuse takes, the time may come when you can no longer tolerate the situation and have to leave immediately. Planning for such an emergency will help you to gain a measure of control over your life and make it easier to cope during a crisis.

First of all, recognise the fact that you do not have to wait helplessly for the next attack – you can plan in advance what you will do. For example, you can confide in a friend and arrange to stay with her if you need to escape in a hurry. You could ask your neighbours to telephone the police if they hear screams for help. If possible, save some money for use in an emergency. You may want to arrange for someone to keep it for you. Find out if there is a refuge nearby which will take you and your children (see chapter 10 for information on refuges). You might feel it would be helpful to tell your children that 'one day, if daddy hurts me, we may have to leave, but it is not your fault if we do'. What you tell your children will depend on their age and emotional state. If you can, without attracting attention, pack a small bag with an essential change of clothing for the children. This way, if there is an emergency, you will not have to worry about what you need in order to leave. (Chapter 11 discusses the children's needs in more detail.) Make a note of a taxi number, find out who has a telephone in the area and/or have money for a public call box. Have a spare set of car and house keys cut and leave them in a safe place. Hide important papers: family allowance and DHSS order books, birth and marriage certificates, passports and cheque/building society books. If you have to escape suddenly it will help to have these documents somewhere where you can reach them quickly. Try working out in advance who you would contact in the event of an attack, such as a woman's refuge, the police or family doctor. Find out how to reach them at any hour of the day or night.

10 Believe in yourself

While it might seem impossible to find solutions to your problems at this stage, it will help if you learn to believe in yourself. If you focus on your own needs, build your self-esteem and become more independent you will come to see that you deserve a better life. You will start believing in your ability to produce positive changes. The mere fact that you can keep on functioning in such a stressful situation shows that you have an exceptional ability to cope.

9 Examining your situation

People who want to help abused women frequently make the mistake of offering them instant solutions. However well intended, telling an abused woman what to do can prevent her from finding a solution that is right for her. What might work for one may not be possible for another. For example, some abused women find it hard to leave their partners for reasons such as economic and emotional dependence, fear of loneliness, and/or lack of accommodation and other resources. Perhaps the solution for some women is talking the problem over with a friend, or admitting to themselves that the abuse exists. For others, the solution will be to create new lives for themselves by leaving their partners. Many abused women who once thought themselves trapped have managed to make the break because someone told them they could get housing and had rights to money from social security. As Janine explains:

I had given up hope . . . . with three kids under five, no money, nowhere to go. My mum would've helped but she wasn't well enough. Then a friend told me there were these places you could go . . . she'd seen it on telly. I went to the CAB and they phoned a battered wives home. I didn't even realise I could get social security.

Remember that whatever choices you make, they are valid. No one else can be you. If you try living up to other people's expectations it is likely that you will be unhappy.

Should you stay or leave?

Many abused women feel guilty and blame themselves for being unable or unwilling to leave their partners. Alison expressed her difficulty:

I know I should leave him. It is what I really want to do. But I just can't seem to make it happen. I don't know which way to turn. Sometimes I think I am to blame, other times I feel angry about the way he treats me. I know he won't change, but I don't know what to do about it. I often come close to leaving, but I panic and wait for something to change. My friends can't understand why I stay. I feel really embarrassed. It is hard to explain. I just feel stuck.

This is a normal reaction to a complex situation. However, this reaction will make you feel more anxious and will lower your self-esteem so that you feel like giving up before you start.

You can change the way you feel and use your energy in a more positive way by remembering that:

- overcoming abuse is a gradual process and can be taken one step at a time; you do not have to make decisions until you are ready;
- carefully considering each option in turn will give you the confidence to get a grip on the situation, whereas getting stuck on the whole question 'Should I stay or leave?' can be too overwhelming;
- even if you are not perfect, your partner is not entitled to abuse you;
- finding a solution takes time and effort, but it is possible.

If you choose to stay in your relationship do not let others make you feel ashamed about your decision. Only you know all the circumstances and how you feel. The object is to stop putting up with abuse, however long it takes you to achieve it.

Drawing up a list of 'pros' and 'cons' is a useful way of clarifying your thoughts about leaving. Talk them over with a friend or neighbour, women's group or even a social worker. Try listing all the arguments for staying in one column, and all the arguments for leaving in another. Your list could include: questions of safety, your feelings and the children's, the effects on your property and finances, the possible consequences for your future. You could try writing out some of the happy/unhappy aspects of the relationship. Consider which ones could happen again and which belong to the past. These lists can help you to discover your feelings about the future of your relationship.

It may be that now is the wrong time for you to focus on the question of staying or leaving your partner. Some women find this question such a heavy burden that their thoughts get weighed down by it. Putting this decision aside for a while will give you the time to think through other issues.

Taking the 10 steps set out on pages 26–32 will help you find an answer to the question 'Should I stay or should I leave?' You may have other anxieties which are troubling you. These are discussed below together with information which will help you to explore your options.

How will you survive without any money?

You may have a real fear of not being able to feed and clothe yourself and/or your children. Do you know about your eligibility for benefits from the Department of Health and Social Security? If you have no money you can claim income support (weekly cash payments from local DHSS benefit offices) so that your basic needs are met. If possible, take along to the benefit offices papers such as birth/marriage certificates, family allowance book, etc.

If your partner is the breadwinner you may be worried about a fall in your standard of living. Ask yourself, is this really worse than the constant fear of abuse? If you do suffer a lowering of living standards this need not be permanent. You could improve your skills or further your education with the aim of improving your job prospects.

Why not start saving for the future even if you don't want to leave now? Saroj put aside £1.50 from the housekeeping money every week for two years and then escaped. Harbijan did piece work, sewing for a clothing company, when her husband was not around. You may, for example, do some babysitting or home typing.

Should you stay for the sake of the children?

Abused women with children have the additional pressure of looking after their children's safety and emotional needs. You may worry that a broken home can only produce 'disturbed children'. Have you considered that an atmosphere of safety, with the love of a single parent, is healthier than the tension and anxiety of an abusive home? A violent father is not a good example for young children to learn from. Children need consistent, reliable adults to depend on, not a violent father. If you are concerned about not having a 'man about the house' or 'father figure' for your children, then think about whether it would be possible for them to form happy relationships with uncles, grandfathers or male friends instead.

Children who witness or experience abuse often suffer the

same damaging effects as abused women, such as low self-esteem, anxiety and/or depression, and physical ailments. Some children who grow up in an environment of abuse go on to repeat the pattern as adults. (See chapter 11 for a more detailed discussion about the effects of abuse on children.)

You may be anxious about depriving the children of a father. Have you considered that living with an abusive man may not be in the children's best interests? Watching you being abused and made unhappy damages their emotional well-being and their sense of security. If you stay, is there a chance your partner will abuse the children? Is it possible that your children could still have a relationship with him even though you no longer live together? Perhaps their relationship may even improve. Remember, just as you aren't responsible for the abuse, you aren't responsible for your partner's failure to live up to the 'happy families' ideal.

If you leave will you be lonely?

It cannot be denied that many women who leave abusive partners experience a painful time of loneliness and uncertainty. However, women can and do recover. Paula found splitting up very hard:

I felt very lonely and conscious of not having anyone to share my good moments with (or bad). Everyone seemed to have a partner. When my sister went to her caravan in Wales I used to go over to be with my niece and take the dogs for walks. I also used to cook for her and prepare meals for their freezer. I used to hate going back to an empty home, but as I had nowhere else to go, I did. Weekends were the worst – life seemed to be about families, when people see their children and grandchildren, and my life seemed pretty bleak without these. My life felt so lonely, as if there was no one and nothing to care for or about.

Things got much better since I started working. Doing the word-processing course was a great boost – learning a new skill at my age [45] seemed a great achievement. Then my boss gave me a high percentage rise. Not everybody got one and I was so pleased. One improvement led to another. I found I had a busy social life and did not miss Phil so much. I even got around to taking tennis lessons. Now there is no stopping me. It certainly was very grim at first, but I knew there was no alternative. He would have destroyed me. Looking back I am so relieved I made the decision I did.

Has it occurred to you that the strength you use to survive the abuse could also be used to cope with loneliness? Many women say that coping with a period of loneliness was better than living with abuse.

Before making up your mind ask yourself how gratifying your relationship is. It is possible you are lonely already within the present situation. The support of friends and relations, or of a women's group, can help reduce the loneliness and give you strength and courage. Have you ever thought you might enjoy your own company and find your independence rewarding? Are you being prevented by your partner from having friends? Many women who have left abusive relationships discover that they are much better at making friends than they thought. Their partner's behaviour had isolated them and made them lose confidence.

If you love him, how can you leave?

However much you love him, will it stop him from abusing you? If you leave, you can keep the memory of a happy love; if you stay, will the abuse embitter it forever? Is your love returned (in actions as well as words)? Does it bring you fulfilment? Is it really love or are you in love with the memories? Are you hanging onto a romantic dream while the facts prove that you are being abused? You may be confusing love with need. If you had enough money, friends, and a comfortable home of your own would your partner still be the only possible man?

You feel sorry for him. Will you ruin his life if you leave?

Already your partner is down. Perhaps he is under great pressure at work, or perhaps he is out of work. Without your support it may seem as if he will fall apart. However, if you leave he may then be motivated to change or get help. An abusive relationship is not healthy for either of you. Will feeling sorry for him change his behaviour, or is feeling pity for him your way of avoiding making decisions about your own life?

How do you know your next relationship won't be worse?

Does this fear mean you should stay in a destructive relationship? Your partner may be holding you back from realising your full potential. Have you thought that when your self-respect is increased you might have a better chance of meeting people who respect you? Is it possible that you could be happy without a man in your life? Women often think of themselves only as somebody's girlfriend or wife. Maybe what your life needs next is independence from men, at least for a while. Building your self-esteem will give you the confidence to take time in choosing the next relationship carefully. Not all relationships are abusive. You will have a better chance, next time, of avoiding an abusive relationship if you take note of the warning signs in chapter 5.

What do you do if it is against your religion to divorce him?

Sometimes people with a strong religious faith feel they have a duty to stay with their partner, or to 'keep the family together'. Some religious leaders forbid divorce or separation. If they were aware of the suffering that abuse causes within some families, perhaps they might encourage women to find peace, even if it meant parting.

There are many interpretations of the great religious scriptures. Is it possible that there are interpretations which respect your right to be safe? Does your religion really require you to live with the misery of violence or abuse? Thinking carefully or praying about these things can help you.

Whatever your religion, some religious leaders will be more understanding than others. If the first person you contact for religious advice is not supportive, it may be worth approaching another.

If you involve the police or go for help will it make matters worse?

Would going for help really be worse than continuing to suffer in silence? Studies show that abuse gets more severe over time.

Have you considered that although going for help may cause distress now, it could prevent a lifetime of misery?

Did you know that assault is a criminal offence? Going to the police may seem like a drastic step to take. However, in some cases it may be necessary to protect yourself. You might want to consider asking the police to charge your partner with assault. Involving the police is also one way of letting your partner know that you will not put up with abuse. Studies in Canada (where the police have a policy of arresting and prosecuting batterers) show that when charges are laid violence is reduced. When charges aren't laid, the violence escalates.[8]

Would revealing the abuse ruin his reputation/career?

Is this just another threat that your partner is using to control you? He may be confusing his personal embarrassment with actual damage to his career. If he was really worried about the effect on his reputation or career, wouldn't he try to change his behaviour, rather than simply cover it up? If his violence against you did harm his position or status, would that have been your fault or his? He is responsible for his actions. How can you take the blame for something which is beyond your control?

It is not your fault if your partner pretends to be an upright citizen but commits assault at home. If other people lose their respect for him when they discover the truth, this is not a problem for which you are responsible.

This chapter has described some of the fears and insecurities women have in an abusive relationship. If you have other concerns that are not mentioned here, try to think them through to make sure you are not deceiving yourself. Remember that there are no simple solutions. Ultimately, it is up to you to stop being a victim of abuse.

If you are to stop being a victim of abuse there are steps to take whether you stay or whether you leave the relationship. The essential first step is to face up to the problem of abuse. The advice in this chapter is aimed at helping you to see your situation clearly, respect yourself and make decisions. To sum up, the most important things to keep in mind are:

- Do not deny that there is a problem.
- Accept that the abuse will not go away until you take constructive action.
- Get help and advice, but make the decisions yourself.
- Do not accept other people's negative judgements about you.
- Respect yourself and build your self-esteem.
- Plan for your safety.
- **Above all, do not blame yourself for the abuse.**

Part III

Solving
the Problem

10 How to get help

Getting help will reduce your isolation, boost your morale, equip you with information and generally give you a stronger foothold on the ladder of independence. Many sources of help are referred to in this chapter. For detailed information on how to contact the main sources of help, please refer to appendix 1.

Remember that advice-giving organisations are run by human beings: some will be sympathetic, some will not. If the people you seek help from appear to be unsympathetic, this probably stems from their lack of awareness of what you have suffered. Even nowadays many people working in the caring professions are just not trained to deal with the problem of woman abuse. They don't mean to be unsympathetic or off-putting, so don't allow yourself to feel disorientated, disillusioned or humiliated by anything they say.

There may be times when you feel it is necessary to be assertive with people such as housing officials or DHSS employees in order to claim your rights; but remember, a quiet, polite but determined approach may be more effective than losing your temper! On the other hand, there are occasions when it is wiser to ignore any unsympathetic attitudes you come across, whilst taking advantage of people's knowledge and expertise. One exception to this is when you are seeking emotional support. If you feel your helper lacks understanding, is too critical, is making unfair judgements or is just too bossy, you are justified in looking elsewhere. Use your common sense to guide you.

Family and friends

Have you ever considered going to friends or family for help and support? Perhaps embarrassment and shame have prevented you in the past. In the long run, the most important thing is that you get the support you need. Your family and friends may even be able to give you a roof over your head.

If you distrust your family and friends then seek help elsewhere. If you are Asian you may be subjected to a great deal of family pressure to stay with your husband. Sunita, who escaped from a violent husband says:

Asian culture is based on traditional views that women are inferior to men and that they are here to bear children and look after the house. They don't get any positive images from their culture unless they cook a good meal or have a son. If a man beats his wife she is expected to put up with it and it is a disgrace for her to leave.

Many Asian women are regarded as social outcasts by their families and friends if they leave their husbands, and therefore it will be necessary for them to find other support. There are refuges for Asian women throughout Britain (see page 46).

Women's refuges

The most valuable resource for a battered woman is a women's refuge. Most refuges encourage women to make their own decisions and take control of their lives. There are hundreds of refuges throughout Britain, set up by different groups. These provide a safe haven for women and children escaping from physical, emotional and sexual violence. They provide accommodation, support and practical advice, including information about schooling, DHSS benefits, housing and facilities available in the local community. Most refuges allow you to stay until you decide what you want to do. Children are welcome (although many Women's Aid refuges will not accept teenage boys.) Some refuges also have special facilities for children such as playgroups, and activities for older children. Even if you do not need accommodation, refuge workers and other women in the refuge will talk to you and help you with your problems. Getting the support of other women and realising that there are many women in your position can be a tremendous comfort. The uniqueness of a refuge is that everyone there understands the meaning of abuse: many of the women there have been subjected to it, so they will know how you are feeling. No one will ask you to tell them the details of your own problems, unless you want to discuss them. Refuges acknowledge that emotional abuse is also extremely traumatic; you will still be helped even if you have not been beaten physically. Some refuges offer follow-up support after a woman leaves.

Places in refuges are in great demand and refuges are therefore often rather overcrowded and noisy, affording little privacy. On the other hand, you will gain tremendous support and reassurance from the presence of other women who have suffered at the hands of abusive men.

Different kinds of refuges are found all over Britain and Ireland. They vary according to who is running them. Generally speaking, there are four types:

Women's Aid refuges

These work on a self-help basis and encourage women to participate in both the daily running of the refuge and in campaigning to prevent woman abuse. The Women's Aid Federation (England) Ltd, Scottish Women's Aid, Welsh Women's Aid and Northern Ireland Women's Aid are funded by the Government to provide and co-ordinate a network of affiliated refuges throughout Britain; there are over 100 Women's Aid refuges in many parts of the UK. The National Women's Aid Federation can give you the telephone number of your nearest Women's Aid refuge (see details in appendix 1). You can also obtain this number from your local citizens advice bureau, advice centre, housing department, social services, marriage guidance counsellor, Samaritans or police.

Independent refuges

These refuges are not affiliated to the Women's Aid Federation, but many of them operate along similar self-help lines. However, a small number of them are run along more formal lines; for example the presence of wardens may mean that women have less say in the daily routine of the refuge. Sometimes there are specialist workers such as housing workers and childcare staff. Although there is no official umbrella organisation co-ordinating independent refuges, there are many of them throughout Britain. You can find out the name and number of your local independent refuge from the organisations listed under Women's Aid above. Also, Chiswick Family Rescue (the first women's refuge in Britain) runs a 24-hour crisis line for women escaping from physical and emotional abuse. They can put you in touch with your local refuge, irrespective of its affiliation (see appendix 1).

Local authority refuges

These are run by social workers and funded by the local council. There are very few of them in Britain. Contact your local social services, town hall, police, or probation service.

Refuges for ethnic minority women

Although no refuge discriminates against minority groups, there are refuges catering specifically for women from ethnic minorities, which offer particular diets, the chance to speak your own language or practise your own religion. Contact your local social services, community relations council, advice centre, police, ethnic minority women's group, citizens advice bureau, Samaritans or marriage guidance counsellors. The National Women's Aid Federation and Chiswick Family Rescue will also be able to put you in touch with ethnic minority refuges (see appendix 1).

Medical back-up

You are strongly advised to get medical help if you have been physically abused by your partner. It can prevent permanent damage to your health and even save your life. What is more, experience has shown that in order to be (a) rehoused, and (b) believed in court, it is vital to have clear medical evidence that you have suffered abuse. Even if your external injuries do not appear to be serious, you may have internal injuries, concussion and/or be suffering from shock.

Hospital

Go to the casualty department. When you arrive, make sure you give the nurses and doctors as much information as possible about what has happened. Good treatment depends on this. If you only tell part of the story you run the risk of serious injuries being overlooked. For example, if you only tell them that your partner has punched you in the face when in fact he has savagely kicked you in the stomach as well, the possibility that you have internal injuries might be overlooked.

Exactly how much information you can reveal may well depend on your circumstances. If your partner has accompanied you to hospital you may be too frightened to speak. Even without your partner's presence, it might be too

upsetting to tell your story. Your physical state could be so
serious that it is not possible for you to talk. However, it will be
helpful if you can:

- discourage your partner from coming into the examination
  room. You have the right to privacy anyway;
- tell the medical staff that it was your partner who injured
  you. If you lie about this, they may be unaware of the full
  implications of your injuries, and the treatment that you get
  may be inappropriate. For example, you may need an x-ray to
  check for broken bones after being punched or kicked;
- give accurate details about the assault. Tell the nurses or
  doctors about the instruments used, about the force and
  direction of any blows, and how long the attack lasted;
- tell the medical staff about any previous injuries caused by
  your partner;
- be sure that there is a record of the full extent of your injuries
  (you may be asked for such evidence later). Most hospitals
  will keep detailed records anyway, but it is helpful for the
  medical staff to know that their evidence might be required
  in court;
- ask the staff to refer you to a social worker, women's refuge or
  the police if you are too frightened to return home. Insist that
  staff keep your new address confidential.

Your GP (family doctor)

Even if you don't feel that you need to go to hospital, it is
essential that you get your injuries recorded. As well as caring
for your health, your family doctor (or the surgery nurse) can
provide medical evidence that you have suffered physical
abuse.

Whether you have been physically, sexually or emotionally
abused, your doctor can also provide practical advice and
support – such as the names of other helpful organisations and
voluntary agencies. Your doctor may also be able to refer you to
a counsellor or therapist. You may need a letter or doctor's
certificate to get sickness benefit or to support your application
for council housing, etc. It is also worth remembering that if
you tell your doctor about the violent situation at home, then he
or she will be better able to understand any problems your
children may have.

If your family doctor is unsympathetic, then try approaching
your health visitor; she might have more time to talk and give
you practical advice. You can get her address and phone
number from your GP or local child health clinic.

Should you involve the police?

The choice is yours whether or not to ask for police help. Bear in mind there will be consequences whatever choice you make.

If you go to the police, they can offer you protection and put you in contact with your local women's refuge. They can temporarily remove the violent man from the home – for example, if they take him for questioning or arrest him. (The only long-term removal would be if he was imprisoned, refused bail or given bail with a condition preventing him from returning home.) If you choose to leave your home they will go back with you if you want to collect your belongings. They can arrange for you to be seen by a doctor and keep a record of the incident for future use. By involving the police you are saying to your partner you will not put up with his violence any longer. If the police arrest him and lay charges against him he will learn that his behaviour has negative consequences. If you find the officers at your local police station helpful, it will make you feel stronger. It will also help you to realise that you do not have to tolerate violence.

If charges are brought against your partner you may have to give evidence about his abusive behaviour in court. This can be a frightening and tiring experience, although your local women's refuge can be very supportive. Remember, you can always ask a woman friend or neighbour to come with you to the police station or court.

Sadly, sympathetic police treatment cannot be guaranteed. If you involve the police and they do little or nothing to help you, then this could leave you feeling helpless and alone, and that there is no one who takes your problem seriously. It may make you reluctant to ask the police for help again. Don't be discouraged – keep trying.

You might decide, for a variety of reasons, not to involve the police. The final decision must be up to you, but think carefully before turning your back on this potential source of help. 'Going it alone' could result in further injury to yourself or your children, or damage to your possessions or property. In addition, keeping the crime secret from the police allows your partner's behaviour to continue unchallenged. Doris involved the police when her fiancé was violent towards her:

I felt a man should not get away with being violent and I hoped that by reporting it to the police this would help other women. The more cases that are reported to the police, the less violence towards women can be ignored.

As an abused woman you are either subjected to your partner's violence or to the risk of receiving rather insensitive treatment from the law. If you can find support and encouragement to help you deal with possible police insensitivity, you will be better off with the law.

Why get police help?

- It is their job to enforce law and order, and protect the public (including you and your children).
- They are available 24 hours a day and can help you in an emergency.
- They should record what happened and take photographs so that there is official proof of your injuries. This can help you secure the resources you need – like housing – to help you start a new life.
- They can transport you to a refuge or hospital.
- Your contact with the police is a way of delivering a firm message to your partner that you will not tolerate abuse and that he has a serious problem. It also shows your children that you will stand up for yourself.
- It sets right the balance of power in your relationship, therefore giving you more control over your life.
- By going to the police now, you are helping your partner in the long run, and possibly even preventing him from murdering you.

What you can expect from the police

Although your partner has committed a criminal offence, the police seldom arrest the violent man and when they do it is usually for another crime; for example, breach of the peace. Generally, women who have approached the police for help have found them unhelpful. In some cases police have sympathised with the violent man and have actually taken his side. Frances, who had been beaten and threatened with a knife, called the police. When they arrived Frances' boyfriend was still in the flat, but it was Frances who was told to 'hush up and be quiet or we will have to take you to the station'. Police sometimes try to get a woman to talk to her violent partner to patch things up, even when the woman explains she is afraid to do this. Ann, for example, was left alone by the police in a room with her violent husband to talk things over. In some cases the police may refuse to help you altogether. Betty – who asked for police help – was told 'we don't deal with domestics at this station'. What is more, black women's groups are worried that if black women contact the police the women will meet racist attitudes.

However, not all police are unsympathetic (especially if you are willing to give a statement), so it is worth persevering. Laura found the police to be helpful and supportive:

They answered my call and removed my violent boyfriend from our flat. I asked them to find me a place in a women's refuge and they even took me and my little boy there.

When the police came to Maria's house she was also treated sympathetically. She had clearly been beaten up.

It was obvious my boyfriend had attacked me, there was blood everywhere. The police interviewed us separately. I would've been too scared to speak otherwise. After they spoke to both of us on our own they arrested Bill. He was charged with actual bodily harm.

Recently the Metropolitan Police issued new guidelines to their officers. The guidelines say that under the Police and Criminal Evidence Act the police have the power to arrest a violent man in order to protect a 'vulnerable person' or child. This includes a woman who has been assaulted or threatened with violence by her partner. However, these guidelines still allow individual officers to make a decision as to whether or not they should arrest. Although it will take time for attitudes to change, training programmes for the police are being undertaken by refuge workers in various parts of the country. It is hoped these programmes will make the police more sensitive and sympathetic to women who approach them. It is too early to say how successful the guidelines and training programmes are proving.

If you ask the police for help and feel they did not treat you properly, you are entitled to register an official complaint against them. To do this you have to write a letter explaining what happened and send it to the Chief Constable for your area. Your local citizens advice bureau or law centre will be able to help you with your complaint.

How to behave with the police

- Above all, try to keep calm so that you can describe as accurately as possible what happened.
- If you would feel happier talking to a woman officer, ask if this would be possible.
- Get the names and constable numbers of the officers who have helped you. Make sure that they keep a record of the incident. This information can be useful if, for example, you need to contact them again.

- Insist on your right to be taken to a women's refuge if you want to go.
- If the police arrest your partner, ask them when he will be released so you can make arrangements for your safety.
- Offer to make a statement for the police to use as evidence in court. Without this they are unlikely to take your accusations against your partner seriously.
- Try and persuade the police to ask for a condition of bail to prevent him from returning home.
- You may want the support of a women's refuge. Ask the police for their telephone number.

The law

The law can help abused women in two ways. Firstly, the police can arrest and charge your partner for committing a criminal offence. Secondly, *you* can take legal action to stop your partner assaulting you; or to regain the right to occupy your home; or to establish custody of your children. To do this, you will need the help of a solicitor and you will probably need to claim legal aid to pay the solicitor's fees and any other charges. You can find out how to contact a sympathetic solicitor, and how to get advice on claiming legal aid, on page 55. You can also see the wide range of legislation which applies to abused women and their rights set out on pages 100–104.

England and Wales

It is a criminal offence for your partner to assault you or to threaten you with violence under the Offences Against the Persons Act 1861, Sexual Offences Act 1956 and Police and Criminal Evidence Act 1984. Possible charges are:

- common assault
- assault occasioning actual bodily harm
- grievous bodily harm with or without intent
- attempted murder
- manslaughter
- rape (If married, only where there is judicial separation, a separation order in the magistrates court, a separation agreement – including a non-molestation clause, a non-molestation injunction or a non-molestation undertaking or a Decree Nisi or Decree Absolute or divorce or Decree of Nullity. In effect, this eliminates the wife's consent to marital intercourse.)

Your partner can also be charged with criminal damage (for example, smashed doors and windows) and breach of the peace.

In cases of domestic violence, the police can and should arrest and charge men for commiting any of the above offences. (Although common assault is not usually an arrestable offence, the police can make an arrest in domestic violence cases (under section 25 (3e) of the Police and Criminal Evidence Act 1984) in order to protect a vulnerable person or child.) It is the duty of the police to investigate crime and take appropriate action. The fact that violence has taken place in the home is irrelevant. You have a right to be protected wherever you are. In reality, however, battered women report that the police are reluctant to bring charges in cases of domestic violence and get involved in family matters.

If the police make an arrest, it is then up to the Crown Prosecution Service to decide whether the case should be prosecuted. The police will automatically refer your case to them for consideration. But you must be prepared to stand by any statements you made to the police at the time of the assault. Without your evidence it is unlikely that the Crown Prosecutor will be successful in proving the case.

Private prosecution

If the police do not arrest your partner, or the Crown Prosecutor is unwilling to prosecute the case, you could initiate a private prosecution. There are disadvantages in doing this: 1) your legal costs would not be covered by legal aid, although the 'green form' scheme (see page 55) would pay your solicitor to give you advice; 2) it is very difficult to pursue a private prosecution without a lot of support and a determined solicitor.

Scotland

A police officer can arrest and charge a man for assaulting a woman providing the officer has credible information that the man committed the crime. The woman herself is the main source of information, backed up by her injuries, signs of a struggle, what neighbours saw or heard and the man's replies to questions. As in England and Wales, the police do not actually prosecute the case. The Procurator Fiscal (equivalent to the Crown Prosecutor in England) will decide whether the case should go to court. Private prosecutions are for all practical purposes not allowed.

Northern Ireland

As in England and Wales, assaulting you or threatening you with violence is against the law (Offences Against the Person Act 1861).

Compensation

Women who have been physically injured by their partners can claim compensation from the Criminal Injuries Compensation Board. The minimum award is £550 but awards of thousands of pounds can be made, depending on the extent of your injuries. You will need to provide proof of the assault, such as a statement from your GP, dentist or the police. You are still entitled to compensation even if the police have not arrested and charged the man with assault. Claiming compensation is not always straightforward and can be very time-consuming. Contact a law centre, citizens advice bureau or solicitor for help in making a claim. While you cannot get full legal aid to cover the cost of claiming compensation, help may be available from a lawyer under the 'green form' legal aid scheme (see page 55 for information on this scheme).

To make a claim get in touch with the Criminal Injuries Compensation Board for an application form (see appendix 1 for the address).

Other legal remedies

If your husband or partner is being violent or threatening you with violence your solicitor can apply to the courts for an order called a 'non-molestation' injunction. An injunction is a written order from the court telling a man to do or not to do certain things such as hit or threaten to hit you and your children. A non-molestation injunction can also be issued for snooping, following you around, interference at work, unreasonable telephoning – for example late at night, frequent humiliation, etc. You will have to prove that this type of behaviour is more than a 'one-off' incident and that it is genuinely upsetting to you.

Injunctions can tell a man to keep away from your home. If you are living together he can be ordered to leave the home and not return so that you and your children can live there. (This is called an 'ouster' order.) Ouster orders are normally only granted for a limited period, usually of not more than three months.

When you ask for an injunction the court will take into account the following details:

- behaviour of your partner, including violence. (The behaviour must have occurred recently so do not delay.) It also includes *your* behaviour, especially if raised by your partner, for example affairs, nagging, etc.
- accommodation available to you and your children and to your partner
- the needs of any children
- why you are asking for an injunction

If the judge is satisfied your partner has caused actual bodily harm to you or your children and will do so again, he or she may attach a 'power of arrest' to the injunction. This means that the police can arrest the man without a warrant if he disobeys the order. Powers of arrest are granted for specific periods only and may need to be renewed. If your partner gives the court an undertaking not to be violent again, the court will often accept such an undertaking rather than attach a power of arrest to the injunction. If you have an injunction without a power of arrest and your partner disobeys it, your solicitor should go back to court and ask for a power of arrest. The judge or magistrate can send your partner to prison for breaking the injunction. (A power of arrest cannot be attached to an undertaking, but it can be enforced by committal to prison, like an injunction.)

If you need an emergency injunction, for example, in cases of extreme danger of violence, your solicitor can apply for an 'ex parte' injunction. This is heard by a judge without your partner being notified, so he will not be in court. It is possible to get emergency legal aid for an ex parte injunction. If you need help to get an ex parte injunction out of normal office hours, contact a women's refuge, law centre or solicitor. You can also ask the local police for the number of an out-of-hours duty judge or High Court judge (in London) who can hear your case. An ex parte order is usually only granted temporarily. If you need the injunction to continue, then notice is given to your husband or partner in the usual way. There is then a further hearing when both parties attend and the question of the injunction is fully considered by the court, unless your partner agrees to it or gives a suitable undertaking. It is extremely unlikely that a power of arrest will be attached to an ex parte injunction. It is important to let the local police know that an injunction has been granted so that they can act effectively if your partner disobeys the order.

Turn to appendix 3 for detailed information on the Acts which provide protection for battered women.

How to find a solicitor

The Law Society publishes a list of solicitors indicating whether they will do work under the Legal Aid Scheme. You can find this list in your local library.

To find a sympathetic solicitor who specialises in housing and family law, ask at a law centre, citizens advice bureau or women's refuge.

Legal Aid

The Legal Aid scheme pays for legal advice and representation at court proceedings for those who cannot afford to pay. You are eligible for legal aid if you are receiving income support from the DHSS or if you have a low income, but your capital (savings) is taken into account in this assessment. Under the Green Form scheme, you can get free legal advice if you qualify, but it does not cover the costs of legal representation. In addition, many solicitors offer a 'fixed fee interview', whereby you can have your first consultation (up to half an hour) for £5.00. Solicitors can help you to apply for legal aid or, if you do not qualify, they can advise you about the costs of taking further legal action.

Scotland

A woman can protect herself from violence in the home by getting an 'interdict' or 'exclusion' order. These court orders are usually obtained from the local sheriff court. Contact a solicitor if you want to apply.

An interdict is a court order prohibiting a person from doing certain things. For example, your partner can be interdicted from molesting, threatening or assaulting you or coming near your home. If you need protection while your application for an interdict is awaiting a hearing, you can apply for an 'interim interdict' which is usually granted immediately and without notice to your partner.

A wife can ask for power of arrest to be attached to an interdict. This enables the police to arrest her husband if he breaks the terms of the interdict. An unmarried woman can have a power of arrest attached only if she and her partner are joint owners or tenants of the home or the court has granted her the right to stay there. A power of arrest can be attached to an interim interdict but your partner has to be given an opportunity to oppose it.

An exclusion order can be obtained under the Matrimonial Homes (Family Protection) (Scotland) Act 1981. Together with associated orders it requires your partner to leave the family home and stops him returning without your permission. As it may take a few weeks before an order is granted, you can apply for an 'interim exclusion order'. Even this takes some days; in the meanwhile you can protect yourself by asking for an interim interdict against molestation or violence. Before the court grants an (interim) exclusion order it must be satisfied that it is necessary to protect you from the conduct of your partner which will injure your physical or mental health. An unmarried woman can apply for an order only if she and her partner are joint owners or tenants of the home or the court has granted her the right to stay there. There is no such restriction for wives. Although you cannot apply for an exclusion order after divorce, the divorce court can give you permission to stay in your ex-husband's house and keep him out of it. If you are the sole owner or tenant of the family home, you can simply tell your violent partner to leave as long as the court has not granted him the right to stay. Where he refuses to leave you can ask the court for an order removing him, by force if necessary. You cannot use this method against your husband.

Inform your solicitor if your husband or partner causes further trouble. For more detailed information you can contact a woman's refuge, housing aid centre or citizens advice bureau.

Northern Ireland

The Domestic Proceedings Order (Northern Ireland) 1980 provides women with protection from their violent partners. Under this legislation you can obtain a protection order to prevent your partner from using violence or from threatening you with violence. You can also obtain an exclusion order which requires your partner to leave the matrimonial home and possibly to stay away from the area you live in. The order is temporary and lasts a specified period, which can be renewable.

A power of arrest can be attached to both these orders. If an order is breached, the police can arrest the man and keep him in custody. However, the police can use their discretion and choose not to make an arrest.

If you need to take action quickly you can apply for an interim exclusion order within 24 hours of assault. The order becomes effective from the time it is served on your husband and usually lasts for up to five weeks. Unmarried women are not entitled to apply for protection under the Domestic Proceedings Order. However you can get an injunction under common law to prevent your partner from using violence against you.

Social services

The local authority employs social workers to help and advise people who are having difficulties with their lives. If you prefer you may be able to see a female social worker and one from your own ethnic background.

Social workers can give you emotional support. They can talk to you to help you clarify your thoughts. They can also give you practical help, such as referring you to a women's refuge, negotiating with the DHSS, schools or housing officials. They may be able to help you find a solicitor and advise you on money problems. If you have children they may be able to give you some money to help you until you can claim from the DHSS.

The quality of help you receive will depend on the individual social worker; unfortunately, not all social workers have sufficient understanding of wife abuse. Their training often teaches them to keep families together and they may advise you to return home. But some social workers may not fully appreciate the physical dangers or the mental damage that going back could cause you. Many abused women worry that their children will be taken into care if they approach social services for help. While it is true that the welfare of children is top priority for social workers, taking children into care should only happen if the children are in danger, and only as a last resort. There are other options available, such as going to a women's refuge or getting an injunction to protect you and the children (see pages 44–46 and pages 53–56).

Money

It is unnecessary for you to stay in a violent relationship because of lack of money. If you have no money you will be entitled to welfare benefit from the state (usually a weekly payment), although the kind of help you receive will depend on your circumstances. For example, you might be entitled to unemployment benefit, income support, sickness benefit, housing benefit and/or single-parent child benefit (normally payable only after a period of separation). The main thing to remember is that you are entitled to benefit to bring your income up to the minimum standard and to help with your housing costs. This applies to any woman living in Britain, unless admitted to the country with limited leave to remain. If you are unsure about your rights and entitlements contact your local citizens advice bureau before making a claim.

If you are not working you can claim income support for yourself and your dependent children. If you are single, unemployed and have no children you can still claim income support but you will have to sign on at an unemployment benefit office saying that you are available for work. It is important to claim as soon as possible because your benefit will usually start from the date you make your claim. If you are in receipt of income support, family credit or have a low income you will be entitled to free legal aid. Working women are entitled to claim other benefits such as housing benefit and family credit.

To calculate your claim for income support, the DHSS will consider you basic requirements (such as rent, food, mortgage repayments, heating, etc.) and deduct any income you receive such as maintenance, child benefit, and income from savings between £3,000 and £6,000, etc. They will then pay the difference between your outgoings and any income you receive. If you have capital in excess of £6,000 you are excluded from claiming income support, family credit or housing benefit, but not child benefit or single-parent addition to child benefit.

If you wish to make a claim, contact your local DHSS office and ask for an appointment. You will need to show the DHSS various documents relating to your claim, such as proof of identity, child benefit book, pay slips, rent book or a letter from a refuge or bed-and-breakfast hotel stating your accommodation charges (see section on housing below).

If you only have limited rights to live in Britain you may not have recourse to public funds. If you make a claim for DHSS benefit you may find that the Home Office will ask you to leave the country. It is therefore advisable to obtain advice from specialist agencies such as the Joint Council for the Welfare of Immigrants or a law centre before claiming benefits.

Housing

Often abused women remain with an abusive partner because they fear they will have nowhere to live. There are several options available:

Temporary accommodation

A women's refuge, bed-and-breakfast hotel or hostel will provide temporary accommodation. If you have children or if you are pregnant, the local council must provide at least temporary accommodation if you are homeless and escaping violence. (See section on local authority housing below.) Often they will place you in a bed-and-breakfast hotel or hostel.

You may prefer the support and safety of a women's refuge. Whilst in a refuge you will probably be given help sorting out more permanent housing. Refuges are non-profit-making organisations. They do make a charge to cover their costs, but don't let the fact that you temporarily have no money deter you from going to one. Refuges will assist you to claim your entitlements.

Whether you are going to a bed-and-breakfast hotel, hostel or refuge, if you have no money you may be entitled to claim income support from the DHSS. If you are working you may be eligible for family credit; even if you are not eligible for these benefits you may be able to claim housing benefit.

Permanent accommodation

You may be eligible for council housing. In some parts of the country, particularly in inner-city areas, there may be an acute housing shortage, and long waiting lists, but do not let that stop you applying for council housing. If your need is really urgent, you may be placed near the front of the queue for rehousing, because applicants on council waiting lists are rehoused according to need. If you are threatened with homelessness or at risk of violence from your partner, you can also be rehoused under the Housing Act 1985 (see below). Apply to your local council's housing department (get the address and phone number from the telephone book), or ask your social worker, women's refuge or citizens advice bureau. Renting from a private landlord is another option, though this is likely to be expensive. The availability of all types of housing varies considerably through the country. If you wish to stay in your home you may consider obtaining an ouster order excluding your partner from the home (see pages 53–56).

If you are married the court can protect your rights to occupy the matrimonial home. If the house is jointly owned there are steps you can take through your solicitor to prevent your husband from selling it without your permission. The court can also decide on a property settlement if you are obtaining a divorce or judicial separation. In England and Wales you have rights of occupation under the Matrimonial Homes Act 1983. Your husband can be ordered to permit you to return to the home.

Only you can decide what is the right course of action. The options you choose will depend on your situation. Housing laws are complex so it is wise to get expert advice from a solicitor, housing advice centre, law centre or citizens advice bureau. There are many good booklets available about housing from organisations such as SHAC, CHAR, etc. (see appendices 1 and 2).

Local authority housing

England and Wales
In England and Wales, if you are experiencing violence you are eligible for housing under Part III of the Housing Act 1985 (previously the Housing (Homeless Persons) Act 1977). You must show you are:

- homeless because of violence
- in 'priority need'
- not intentionally homeless

If you become homeless, threatened with homelessness and have a priority need, the local authority have a duty to provide temporary accommodation until they have investigated your circumstances. You have a 'priority need' if you are pregnant, have dependent children or are vulnerable. Because of the scarcity of council accommodation, many local authorities may pressure you to provide proof of violence. They may also ask you to get an ouster order to exclude the man from the home and then suggest you can return as you are no longer at risk. You do *not* have to do this, so contact a solicitor or law centre before agreeing. If you are rehoused under the Housing Act 1985 you will be made one offer of accommodation by the council. Often the accommodation will be of a poor standard. If you feel the accommodation offered is unreasonable, *do not reject it* without first speaking to your local law centre, housing advice centre or women's refuge, or you may spoil your chances of getting a second offer. The council as landlord is responsible for repairs; in some circumstances you can get material from the council to do the redecorating yourself. If the council have a duty to provide temporary or permanent accommodation, they are responsible for storing your property and ensuring that it does not become damaged or stolen.

Scotland

In Scotland a woman has an automatic right under the Matrimonial Homes (Family Protection) (Scotland) Act 1981 to stay in her husband's home even when he tries to sell it or give up the tenancy. Unmarried women have to apply to the court for the right to stay.

If you have the right to stay in the home, the 1981 Act allows you to apply to the court for an order transferring the tenancy (private landlord or council) from your husband or partner to you. In the case of a council tenancy you can ask the council to use their powers under the Tenant's Rights Etc. (Scotland) Act 1980 to get it transferred to you. An unmarried woman does not have to apply to the court for the right to stay in order to approach the council. This procedure can also be used after divorce. If you are escaping violence from your partner you can also apply for rehousing under the Housing (Homeless Persons) Act 1977. As in England and Wales, you will have to show that you are:

- homeless or threatened with homelessness
- in priority need
- not intentionally homeless

The council must see that you are provided with suitable permanent accommodation. The council may ask you to get an order to remove your partner from the home or to prohibit him from behaving violently towards you so that it will be safe for you to remain there. You should not agree to this without contacting your solicitor, citizens advice bureau or law centre.

Northern Ireland

There is no homeless persons' Act in Northern Ireland. Women escaping violence can apply for rehousing from the Northern Ireland Housing Executive, but a decision to rehouse you depends on the discretion of your local officer. Once a decree of divorce is granted, the court can order that a property be transferred from the husband's name into the wife's name or make an order giving a wife and children permission to live in the home even if it remains in the husband's name.

For more detailed advice on your housing rights you should contact a solicitor, law centre or housing advice agency.

Other sources of help

Practical help

You may need information on housing, income support, divorce, separation, custody, immigration and citizenship. The following agencies offer specialist help and advice: citizens advice bureaux, law centres, housing advice centres, SHAC, Shelter, the Child Poverty Action Group and Rights of Women (see appendix 1). If you are not a British citizen, your right to remain in this country may be affected if you leave your husband. It is advisable to consult a solicitor or organisation which specialises in immigration and citizenship regulations. The Joint Council for the Welfare of Immigrants can help you with this (see appendix 1).

If you are an ethnic minority woman you may need an interpreter. For names of reliable interpreters contact a women's group such as the Black Sisters in Southall, London, or a law centre. Asian women's refuges are also a valuable resource (see page 46).

Emotional help

Trying to solve the problem on your own can be stressful. You may need emotional support, counselling and/or therapy to help you make decisions. This kind of help reduces your isolation and helps clarify your thoughts (see step 3 on getting help, pages 26–27).

There are many organisations providing emotional help. Refuges and rape crisis centres offer a confidential counselling service for abused women. Talking things over with other women in a refuge can help you realise you are not alone and that women can and do recover from abuse. Refuges and rape crisis centres do not charge for their advice and counselling services (see appendix 1 for information on how to contact your local refuge/rape crisis centre).

You may also feel that you need longer-term support and professional help. To do this, you need to find a therapist or counsellor. Some therapists and counsellors work on a professional basis (i.e. you pay them a fee), others work voluntarily, and still others can be contacted via the National Health Service. Ask your General Practitioner/family doctor to refer you. Appendix 1 will give you details of how to contact different types of therapists.

The best way to find a therapist is through personal recommendation: from a friend, doctor, health visitor or social worker. Many therapists advertise in the local press, but it is advisable to ask the therapist for his or her qualifications and experience before accepting advertisements. Fees should be negotiated beforehand; many therapists will reduce fees for people on low incomes. If you do not feel comfortable with a therapist, for example, because she or he suggests you are somehow to blame for the abuse, then try someone else.

Finding a therapist is more difficult if you live outside London. You could telephone the national counselling/therapy organisations for the number of someone in your area (see appendix 1).

Do not be intimidated by therapists who are highly qualified, with a string of letters following their name. If their unsympathetic approach makes you feel uncomfortable, go elsewhere for help. Watch out for unacceptable questions from them, such as the following:

- What did you do to provoke him?
- Do you secretly enjoy violence?
- Why did you choose a violent relationship?
- Perhaps he abuses you because of the drink?
- Were you paying enough attention to him?
- Maybe he was under stress at work?

Comments like these show a lack of understanding about what you have gone through. People who do not understand the nature of woman abuse cannot help you. They can only add to your problems by making you feel more isolated, guilty, ashamed and worthless.

Someone may suggest that you and your partner receive counselling together. This may sound like a good idea, but it does not work unless your partner has already recognised that he has a problem and has taken steps to get help for himself first. If he does not take responsibility for his actions, there is a danger that (a) he will abuse you after the counselling session and (b) he will manipulate both you and your helper into believing it is *you* who must change. Spending your time continually justifying and modifying your behaviour is not only counter-productive, it undermines you as well.

Look for a counsellor who can understand what you have been through and who can help you, sympathetically, to discuss your pain and your feelings of helplessness and confusion. Do not let anyone blame you for the abuse or push you to making decisions you are not ready to make.

If you cannot afford to pay for therapy or counselling try talking to workers at a women's refuge, social workers, marriage guidance counsellors, the Samaritans or a priest. There are several organisations offering support to one-parent families, such as Gingerbread, Parents Anonymous, Organisation for Parents Under Stress, Family Network. Their services are free of charge.

11 What about your children?

Children have an amazing capacity for survival, but growing up in a home where their mother is being abused can make a misery of their childhood and damage them emotionally. As helpless onlookers in an abusive home they are affected deeply. They live in an emotional war-zone, often caught in the cross-fire. These emotional battles breed confusion, fear and anxiety. This does not mean that your children will become disturbed or that they will be permanently damaged. With encouragement you can help them to recover from the pain they have experienced.

How does abuse affect your children?

Through their parents children absorb values and attitudes, and learn how to behave. Children are extremely receptive to the emotional atmosphere of their surroundings. If there is violence in the home children may grow up believing this is the way adults behave. Unless they are provided with alternatives for comparison they will begin to think that their parents' violent behaviour is normal. Such children may be unable to build their self-esteem and develop a sense of identity. If their emotional development and well-being are dependent upon parents who are in constant conflict, they become insecure. They feel that they have no reliable adult to turn to. In seeing their father lose control and their mother unable to do anything about it, they feel isolated, fearful and confused. In abusive homes children often harbour fears that they are not lovable, that they do not deserve happiness. This can make them lose trust, fear abandonment and become defensive.

Often children believe that they are to blame for the abuse, but they don't understand why. They feel ashamed and embarrassed, and think that they are missing something compared with their friends who come from happy homes. Sometimes they feel anger towards their father for abusing, and anger towards their mother for allowing it to happen. Some children begin to accept abuse as normal. A male social worker visiting a refuge playgroup was profoundly shocked by one three-year-old's reaction to seeing him. She cowered and said: 'You're not going to hit me are you?'

Sometimes children learn to use violence themselves. Over time sympathy for their mothers can turn into indifference and resentment. Constantly anticipating trouble, they become bewildered, and alternate between feelings of guilt and anger. Outwardly, these feelings are expressed as hostility, rebelliousness and physical aggression. Inwardly, they are shown by withdrawal, depression, self-destructive behaviour and even suicide.

Sometimes a man will not stop at abusing his partner and goes on to abuse his children. A violent man may even sexually assault his children. Sometimes a woman is so overwhelmed and frustrated by abuse that she takes her feelings out on her children.

Children show different responses to abuse in the home. For instance, one might respond by becoming violent. Another might reject violence altogether. However, all children in abusive homes are under stress. Living with this kind of stress can leave the child scarred: emotionally, psychologically and physically. The extent of the damage depends on how resilient the child is. Symptoms of stress can take any of the following forms:

- withdrawal
- aggression
- bullying
- tantrums
- vandalism
- problems in school
- truancy
- hindered learning
- speech problems
- stammering
- attention seeking such as clowning about, distracting other pupils
- accident proneness
- bedwetting
- headbanging
- nightmares
- insomnia
- anxiety
- depression
- fear of abandonment
- feelings of inferiority
- drug or alcohol abuse
- glue sniffing
- eating disorders
- constant colds
- headaches
- ulcers
- asthma and other physical ailments

- mutilation and killing of pets
- running away from home
- suicide attempts

While some of these reactions are normal for any growing child, children from abusive homes are particularly susceptible to these symptoms of stress. Although they may worry you, be reassured that it is possible to overcome them, so that emotional harm to your children is not permanent.

What can you do?

How can you undo the harm and begin the healing process? Above all remember that having a strong and confident mother to learn from is a great encouragement for a child. The more self-reliant you are, the more secure your children will feel.

Be honest with your children

Children are able to detect problems very easily. It is more reassuring for a child to be told the truth than not to understand what is going on. If they are not given an honest account of the situation they will become confused between the lies you tell them (which they would like to believe), and the evidence of their eyes and ears. They already know that they are living under difficult circumstances, but unless they know the truth they cannot deal with this knowledge. Covering up will create anxiety and mistrust. The more honest you are, the more confident your child will be.

This does not mean you have to explain every detail. You could say for instance. 'Your dad and I are having some problems. I don't want to talk about them now, but I want you to know that this is not your fault', or 'Your dad and I have been fighting a lot recently. Don't worry though, I am going to get help.' Be sure to follow this with some reassuring gesture such as a hug or cuddle. Giving your child honest information provides stability and strengthens the bond between you. Children will find it easier to cope with the situation if you tell them the truth. Although you may not feel in control of the situation your children will feel you are. This is turn will give you extra strength to take charge of your life.

Tell them it is not their fault

Children tend to feel responsible for any problems their parents may have. It is therefore vital to tell them that this is not the case. They are not to blame for someone else's behaviour. If they are led to believe they are responsible, they will carry a heavy burden of guilt. For instance, saying to your children, 'I am only staying for your sake' would make them feel that things would be better if they were not around. As a result, they see themselves as unwanted. Guilt will make them feel helpless and contribute to any feelings of worthlessness the abuse might already be causing.

Teach them that abuse is not acceptable

It is important to explain to your children that it is not right for your partner to abuse you. Teach your children that there are more acceptable ways of dealing with anger and frustration. Show your children that you believe this by setting a strong example yourself. Follow the steps on pages 26–29 such as getting help and building your self-esteem.

Help them discuss their feelings

Bottling up their feelings puts children under enormous pressure. Repressed feelings fester into guilt, anger and anxiety. On the other hand, providing a sympathetic ear when they want to talk can only be beneficial.

It is likely that your children will feel angry and frustrated. If you make them feel loved, understood and accepted, they will feel much freer to talk about their anger and fear. You can do this by listening to your children and by responding to their feelings with respect and understanding. This will reduce their anxiety and make them feel more confident and secure. Ultimately, they will come to realise that violence is not a healthy way to deal with frustration, but that expressing their feelings and talking through any problems is much better.

Avoid burdening them with adult responsibilities

Tell your children the truth of your situation, but do not expect them to mother you. Relying on them for the help and support you would get from a close friend can place an unreasonable pressure on them. It can make them feel worried that you are helpless. As they are not in a position to solve your problems, they too may feel helpless. Children who have been forced to behave as adults may be deprived of their childhood. Helping with the chores is a part of learning, but expecting children to run the household is an unfair burden. So is asking them to share your emotional problems.

Encourage them to mix with other people

Contact with other people will make your children feel less isolated and boost their confidence. They may find it difficult to relax and feel secure at home, but mixing with others will help to give them a sense of belonging. If they see peace and harmony elsewhere they will have a yardstick by which to measure their personal growth. By letting them share in happy relationships outside the home, they will learn that not all people behave destructively towards one another.

Help them to stay safe

Often children are the most serious casualties of woman abuse. Seeing their mother attacked, children naturally want to stop it happening. Sometimes they try to come between their parents to stop the violence. Usually the result of this intervention is that the children receive injuries as well, and the physical damage to them may be worse.

The experience of many battered women shows that a more effective way for the children to stop the violence is for them to go for help by phoning the police or fetching neighbours or relatives. Warn your children of the dangers of intervening when your partner is out of control. Tell them they are not responsible for protecting you and that it is all right for them to leave you. By going to a women's refuge not only will you protect yourself, but your children will also be safe.

Teach them to reach out for help by doing so yourself

Your partner may try to make you and the children feel that letting outsiders know about the violence brings shame on the family. Teach your children that getting help is a positive step to take. Let them know that it is the violent behaviour which is shameful. The family can bear embarrassment, but violence could destroy it. Your children will realise there is nothing to be ashamed of, provided you have set an example by informing key people – such as neighbours, teachers and/or relatives – of the situation. Tell your children that you have advised these people about the problems at home. Encourage them to seek help from them at any time.

Build their self-esteem

If you have become preoccupied with the problems of living with abuse, your children's needs may have been overlooked, resulting in a loss of their self-esteem. However drained you feel, even a little encouragement goes a long way to boost your children's self-esteem. Self-esteem is not big-headedness. People with high self-esteem have a healthy love and respect for themselves, and consequently towards other people. If children grow up believing they deserve respect they will be more likely to invite positive responses from others, and vice versa. If they value themselves they will value other people. The more positive messages your children receive at home, the more competent they will be at handling life outside. Furthermore, self-esteem is the most powerful armour against the destructive effects of living in a troubled family.

How can you build your child's self-esteem?

Avoid telling your children that they are bad or that they are stupid. Correct them by saying that what they have done is wrong *without* implying that they are bad people. If you tell them that their *actions* are wrong they can improve by changing what they do. Being labelled 'bad children' lands them with the task of changing who they are, before they can earn your approval.

Avoid comparing your children with others. Comparisons can lead to feelings of inferiority, jealousy, envy and competitiveness. If children think that their value depends on achieving more than others, they may never even attempt a new challenge. Getting pleasure from their own achievements, regardless of how well anybody else is doing, is a key to making progress.

Praise your children. This helps to give them self-confidence. Passing on compliments, by letting them know when other people have said nice things about them, also helps. Taking time to listen to your children lets them know that they are valued.

Let your children know you love them. Loving mothers sometimes do not tell their children that they love them because they assume their children know. The more children feel loved and understood the better they will be able to cope with the problems at home.

Encourage their interests. This helps children to develop an identity and build their self-esteem. Your encouragement shows that you respect them.

Practical considerations

Access

Custody and access – that is, the right to care for and control, and the right to have regular contact with, your children – are complex issues and you should seek the advice of a solicitor or law centre if any dispute arises between you and your partner regarding your children.

Provided you are married both parents have certain 'parental rights'. You have the legal right to take your children with you if you decide to leave. However, your husband is also entitled to have them. Therefore, if your marriage breaks up it would be wise to apply through a solicitor for what is known as interim custody until the long-term custody of the children is sorted out. This usually happens as part of divorce or judicial separation proceedings or under the Guardianship of Minors Act if you are not married, or married and not getting divorced. If you apply for interim custody, your husband may decide to apply for access or custody. He has a legal right to see his children unless there is a good reason for him not to (the court will have to be convinced of this). In the majority of cases, the woman is awarded custody of the children, and the husband is allowed 'reasonable access' to them. If your husband is granted access there may be a risk of further violence as he will be able to obtain your new address either from the court or from the children. Access can create additional problems especially for black and Asian women who are often subjected to considerable community and family pressure to return to a violent man.

If you are worried that your partner will take the children from you or take them abroad without your consent, you can have them made wards of court, or apply for an injunction (interdict in Scotland) preventing their removal. You can do this even if your children are living with their father. Ask a solicitor what steps you need to take.

If you are not married to the children's father he does not have an automatic right to custody or access. If he wants to see his children, and you don't want him to, it will be necessary for him to obtain a court order.

On rare occasions courts make arrangements for supervised access at a safe place such as social services or probation departments. This is because in certain cases it might be unadvisable for the children to visit their father alone. They may need another adult to go along to protect them. You yourself might be in physical danger when handing the children over, in which case arrange, or ask the social services to arrange, for someone else to do this.

Whether your separation is temporary or permanent the thought of your children seeing their father may cause you considerable anxiety. You may fear further violence when you hand the children over, or that they might become distressed at seeing him again, or that he might exploit the opportunity to manipulate you psychologically and emotionally. Whatever the problems in your relationship, it is important that the children are not used as weapons. Respect their right to see their father, unless this would put them in danger or cause them serious distress.

If you have a valid reason for not allowing your children to see their father (for example, you fear he will be violent with them, or feel that he is not capable of looking after them) you can go to court to have the access order withdrawn. Make sure your children understand why you have taken this action.

Children are sometimes very unsettled after access visits. Your partner may have complained about you or tried to get information from them. Dealing with your children's feelings after seeing their father requires patience and understanding. Do not expect your children to act as mediators and try not to question them yourself. They cannot resolve the problems between you and your partner. Above all do not criticise their father in front of them. This makes them feel guilty and confused. They may have strong feelings of love for their father but are afraid of betraying you. Respect their feelings. Let them know that you understand their desire to keep in touch with him.

If you have to leave your partner, it is preferable to take your children with you if you can. Once you have left them it is harder to get them back. However, very occasionally a situation may arise where you have to leave your partner without taking your children. This may make you feel guilty, but remember you cannot tackle your childrens' problems until you have faced your own. By strengthening yourself first you will be in a better position to help your children, and to fight to get them back if need be.

Schooling

When life at home is disturbing this will probably be reflected in a child's life at school. Effects of violence at home can show themselves in different ways. Schoolwork may suffer. The child may become silent and withdrawn, or noisy and disruptive in class. On the other hand, some unhappy children become obsessive over-achievers and become desperately anxious if they are not top of the class.

A child's behaviour outside the classroom will be affected too. Some children bully others; some withdraw and have no contact with others; some will do anything to be noticed, whether it is naughty, dangerous, or just silly; some will lie and steal; some will invent fantastic stories about themselves.

Teachers faced with anti-social behaviour will usually want to protect the other children by stopping the disruptive behaviour. Teachers may punish the child if they think that naughtiness is the cause. If bottled-up unhappiness is the root cause of the child's behaviour this will only make matters worse. It may help to let your child's teacher know that there are problems at home. However, you may not want to reveal details of these problems to the school even though you have nothing to be ashamed of. If this is the case, you could make a general statement such as 'If you are having difficulties with our child it may be because things are not going well at home.' The teacher can then take constructive action such as giving the child individual attention in class or taking pressure off the child.

Leaving your partner may mean your children have to change schools, which can unsettle them at first. Explaining the background to the teacher will help. If you are staying in a refuge the workers there usually liaise closely with the schools and can act on your behalf. Teachers frequently offer support and advice on how to help your child, or put you in touch with someone who can.

Counselling

Showing some signs of distress is a normal reaction for a child in a home where there is abuse. Rushing your children to professional advisers may give them the feeling that there is something wrong with them or that *they* are causing problems.

However, if you follow the key points listed on pages 66–69 above and your child continues to show excessive symptoms of stress, you might consider asking for professional help for your child, for example, from a social worker, child psychologist, family therapist or child guidance counsellor. You could also ask these people for advice on how you yourself can help the child. Your doctor or local social services may be able to refer you.

There are many organisations offering support and advice such as Parents Anonymous, Gingerbread, Childline and women's refuges (see appendix 1 for how to get in touch). If you take your children for professional help remember to reassure them that they are not to blame for the problems in the family. That way emotional scars will heal more quickly.

12 Coping with change

However much you look forward to making changes, the reality of making the break from an abusive relationship can seem hard. Changes in your life may produce waves of emotion. The great relief you feel at having escaped from an abusive man is clouded by overwhelming loneliness. New opportunities fill you with excitement but fear of independence dampens your enthusiasm. Because your children seem unsettled, your firm belief that one reliable parent is better than two warring parents becomes weakened. Sometimes your feelings alternate between certainty and uncertainty: 'Have I made the right decision?', 'Will my life get better?', 'Why don't I feel happy?', 'What will the future hold?' You may feel bitterness and resentment: 'Why am I alone after all I have done to make the relationship work?' if you have stayed with your partner you may ask, 'How will he react to the changes? Will I still love him? Will the relationship be tolerable?'.

Whether you are married or single, these are typical questions for any women to ask herself. Making changes involves taking risks and letting go of the old, familiar past. This seems scary at first. For a while you may even feel worse. You may think you are the only person going through such a difficult time – other people around you seem so happy and satisfied. People may seem not to understand your pain. They may shrug it off or tell you that, over time, you will forget your partner. But there are many people – doctors, nurses, counsellors, refuge workers and other abused women who understand your feelings and will help you cope with them.

However unsettled or uncertain you might feel, don't let that stop you leaving an abusive man once you have decided that's what you want to do. There are ways of coping with change. You may eventually learn to enjoy it, and come to see the time when you broke with the past as a new and exciting period of your life. Although you cannot predict the future, don't be frightened by it. Believe in yourself, in your strength and abilities, and in your right to a life free from abuse. Following the guidelines below will help you to cope with the changes in your life, and look forward to the future.

Trust yourself

Making changes is like laying down all the burdens you have been carrying, so that you have both hands free to get hold of life. Having done this, all you may be able to see is your empty hands. You may become so anxious to fill them up again that you would rather go back to the old unhappy relationship than experience the discomfort of the unknown. Freeing yourself from the past may be the most difficult hurdle to overcome. The temptation to run back to the familiar may be overwhelming. It may seem easier to ignore the reality of yesterday and find excuses for your partner's behaviour. It is a common pattern for a man who abuses his partner to show great remorse after an abusive incident.

Margaret believed her partner's promises to change. Having left him once she gave him another chance. She went back and quickly realised what a mistake this was. Her decision to leave had been right in the first place:

After all the harm he had done to me, I still gave him a chance to prove how genuine his remorse and sorrow were. He threw away that chance when he complained about 'spending a whole day on my affairs'. This was after spending days on what he wanted to do . . . a couple of days round the charity shops, a ploughman's lunch at the pub, Guinness together several evenings at the Working Man's club, three 'exciting' Saturdays at jumble sales, then a shout-up in the car because I dared interrupt. Now, in the last few weeks, with my eyes wide open, I have been able to look at the true situation.

If you have left your partner you may experience terrible loneliness at times. This can make you panic and wonder if you will ever cope. During this period of change, try to remember that feelings of discomfort and desperation are normal. On the other hand, your determination to change your life for the better means that you are freer to seize good opportunities as they come your way. But don't panic if you don't immediately feel full of confidence and energy and don't be frightened into thinking that someone else is better at looking after your life than you are. There may be an initial period where you feel anxious. Letting go of the past is frightening, but if you persevere you will adjust to your new situation. By trusting yourself and using your judgement you will get a firmer grip on the future.

Take one day at a time

The road to self-determination and self-respect may seem long, but the secret is to inch yourself along slowly. Joy describes this feeling:

When I first walked out on Trevor, I felt really terrified he'd come after me and kill me. He was big, broad, massive and large – I knew if he come after me I'd had it. He was obsessed, you know, with controlling his woman.

Suddenly I was free and I didn't know how to handle it. I was like a zombie, you know, being dead skint, black, a woman . . . you feel so vulnerable. Then I started going to church again and the good Lord he helped me. Each day I got the strength to carry on. Now I'm back on my feet.

Plan for your new life carefully, and follow your own pace. If for example, impatient relatives say, 'Why on earth can't you just forget him and get on with your life?', do not be put off. You cannot possibly make all the changes at once. In fact, by making changes slowly and methodically you will build a firmer footing for the new you. Each achievement will give you more confidence and energy. Live in the present, take one day at a time. Of course, in the back of your mind you will know there are many problems to solve, but don't be overwhelmed by all that you have to do.

Angela said:

I've even secretly bought a flat for myself. I know it's daft but I feel really ashamed for staying and yet overwhelmed at the thought of leaving him. I am still with him three years later.

Jill could not face the thought of leaving her partner:

I want to make a go of the relationship. He can be so loving and caring sometimes. He says he loves me and can't live without me. I know his bad side will come again so I've told the doctor about the problems. I felt really embarrassed at first, but she was so nice and even arranged for me to see a therapist.

By focusing on the present, you can deal with one problem at a time. The main thing is to get started on planning your new life without your abusive partner and not to worry about how much you can or cannot do. Every achievement, however small, will make you feel more positive. Gradually you will be able to recognise and grasp new opportunities when they arise and your self-confidence will grow.

Have realistic expectations

We all want to be happy, to feel we have accomplished something and to be successful. But any changes you make in your life will have positive and negative aspects. Try not to let these highs and lows take you over. Keep an even keel. Don't float off on a cloud of enthusiasm in case the difficulties bring you back to earth with a bump. If you feel too many lows, remember the good things that are happening and review your ever-growing list of accomplishments. Above all have realistic expectations. Timna says:

When I look back on all those wasted years I think I must've been crazy to stay with him. At the beginning it was so hard, being on my own and all that. I felt this terrible emptiness. I could barely cope from one day to the next, but it got easier over time and now all my friends say I'm a different person. I look and feel 10 years younger. I felt half dead with all that fear of being under his control. Now I really feel alive and happy. It was an effort, but, my God, I'm so happy I'm not with him anymore.

Remember that life is not always fair, nor is it easy. Don't give up if you notice yourself feeling low. Many abused women who have started new lives for themselves have said that there are low periods, but they do pass. Making a new life for yourself does not happen overnight. It requires hard work, but you can do it.

Keep healthy

Getting plenty of exercise, relaxation and rest will help you to respond better to the stress of change. Louise still lives with her partner, but has managed to make certain changes in her life:

I'm still not sure what the future holds, but I live in the present. I've found it helpful having a counsellor to talk to and my new job makes me feel more independent. One thing that's great is that I've joined an exercise class with the girls at work, and I've got pretty fit. John gets very jealous of my contacts with people, but so far he's not got out of hand. I still get jumpy sometimes wondering what state he's going to be in, but then I think, well – if I look after myself – at least I can cope better.

At times you may feel that the last thing you want to do is go out and get some exercise, but remember, the better you feel physically the better you will feel emotionally. For instance, you could join a keep fit/exercise class, swim, or take walks in the park. Try to get some fresh air and plenty of sleep. Eat nourishing food. Use your solitude to pamper yourself (enjoy lying in a hot bath, watch a film in bed, knit or sew something for yourself). If you are fit you will have more stamina – you need all the strength you can get.

Build contacts outside the home

When you are involved with an abusive man, you often start to see yourself through the distorted mirror of your partner's hatred and scorn. Under these circumstances, it is very difficult for you to see the true you. Lorraine said:

I was just so run down and depressed. He kept telling me what a useless slut I was, I couldn't do anything right so I stopped bothering. It was a vicious circle. The beatings got worse. After a while I couldn't even be bothered to wash my hair. I looked a right sight. Then one day I bumped into an old school friend on the stairs. She'd moved into one of the other flats in our block and we got talking. She made me realise that there was more to life.

Your response to change is largely determined by how you see yourself. Confidence in your own strength and a real determination to improve your lifestyle will help you make positive changes.

If being alone frightens you, you have three choices:

- to stay with/go back to your partner
- to find another person to depend on (that is, start a new relationship on the rebound)
- to develop your own talents and learn to depend on yourself for the moment.

Going back to your partner may leave you with the abuse. Finding another person to depend on while your self-esteem is low will probably lead you to make the wrong choice out of desperation. Developing your talents and learning to rely on yourself will help you, whether you decide to find a new relationship or not. With increased self-respect you have a better chance of being respected by your next partner. Building contacts outside the home will help you to overcome loneliness, boost your self-esteem, develop new skills or interests and gain confidence.

A good 'supportive system' of family and friends can help you to move away from feeling dependent on your partner and frightened to act without him. Many women who have survived abusive relationships say they benefited from joining a women's group. This can help to reduce your isolation and restore your sense of self-respect. Meeting new people can bring you fulfilment, but it is important that you do not become dependent on them. Be careful, too, to choose new friends who accept you as you are, and who will treat you as an equal. If you socialise with people who criticise you all the time, their criticisms will add to your partner's, and double your feelings of worthlessness. Try mixing with people who build your self-esteem, show understanding of (not pity for) your situation, and encourage you to attend to your own needs.

Develop your interests

Developing interests and new activities can do wonders and begin to fill the gap in your life. For instance you can

- discover hidden abilities and inner strengths
- become more competent at making decisions
- feel more confident to take charge of your life
- become more independent. (If you build your capacity to be independent, you are more likely to establish a healthy relationship with a new partner.)
- feel more alive

It will take time, but by exposing yourself to new interests and experiences you will discover you have the power to improve your life. Although Dawn did not leave her partner, her life brightened after she joined a women's group:

I found I had a lot to offer and share. I felt a tremendous release at being able to talk freely with other women. It was as if I had been sealed up in a parcel all this time and then the strings had been undone.

You can start by developing your skills, enrolling in a course, taking up a sport, or finding a job. Colleges of further education offer many kinds of courses including word processing, cake decorating, car maintenance, self-defence, do-it-yourself workshops, foreign languages or fine arts. If you are interested in starting a business your local Job Centre can give you advice about the schemes that are available. You might try doing some voluntary work or campaigning for a political party.

The main thing is that you develop interests which you find stimulating and which will increase your self-confidence. This way, the temptation to return to your partner or repeat old patterns of dependence will be reduced.

The fear of change may slow you down at first, but if you follow the advice above, you will find that taking control of your life, and deciding what you want to do with it, gets easier and easier. Sarah changed her life completely:

Leaving my partner was the most difficult decision of my life. I didn't want to leave, but I knew I had to or he would destroy me. I felt numb at first, but I stuck with my decision. At times I was so lonely I could hardly stand it. Seeing my friends and doing things I liked to do helped. Sundays were the worst days. Everyone else seemed to be happy and in love, walking hand-in-hand. I felt so alone, but I knew returning wasn't an option. My husband was really dangerous. So I decided I had to pull myself together. I took up swimming and aerobics. I entertained my friends for the first time. Eventually I started an Open University course and now I have a good job in publishing. Recently I put down a deposit for a flat. I feel proud of my accomplishments. I am relaxed and in control of my life. I don't have to look over my shoulder and wonder when Steve is going to lose his temper. I was very hurt by the break-up, but I have survived. I had to scrape and crawl my way out of the relationship, but it was worth it. I could never live that way again.

The following story shows how Balraj changed her life, despite tremendous resistance from her traditional Asian family:

I came over to this country to get married. It was an arranged marriage. I did not meet my husband before our wedding day. It was terrible from the start. He was brutal on our wedding night. He drank too much and started beating me after I gave birth to our first daughter. My in-laws said he was violent because I had a girl instead of a boy. The beatings occurred almost daily. After 15 years of marriage the police helped me escape to a woman's refuge. My relatives found out where I was and tried to persuade me to go back, but I knew he was capable of killing me. I couldn't speak English. I was terrified of living on my own in a strange country. My husband refused to let me go to the market so I had no idea of how to shop or do things on my own or learn to speak the language. The workers in the refuge gave me lessons and the English women in the refuge were very kind. After nine months I was offered a house by a housing association. I was frightened to be on my own. My relatives found out where I was and they threatened to burn my house down and kidnap my children if I didn't go back to my husband. My husband

*turned up on the doorstep all the time and I had to call the police
many times. Once my husband smashed his way into the house and
broke my thumb. My children were frightened too. The rest of the
Asian community ignored me. They called me names in the street.
My own family in India wrote and said they would never forgive me
for leaving my husband.*

*They were wrong. I am glad I did not give in to them. I have my
own life now. I have been free for five years. If I had stayed with him
I am sure he would have killed me. I have learned English, and I
have learned how to drive. Every week I go to a support group for
Asian women who have left their husbands. It is especially difficult
for Asian women, but I want to help others to get free like I did.*

Margaret had had all she could take. She wrote about her
experiences:

*He can no longer brainwash me into believing 'I am the meanest,
most selfish, hard-hearted person.' No longer will I put up with
sudden, unexpected attacks from a man I have loved and trusted.
Being subjected to a nightmare ordeal by him heightened my awareness. It is not that I am being 'stubborn and vindictive' as he claims,
I'm just not putty anymore; I'm a different person after my latest
ordeal. This time smooth talk didn't get me straight back into his
kitchen. I'm no longer a yo-yo on his string. No longer will I be
shouted at while driving or kicked out of the house in mid-winter
with half an hour's notice and no time to pack warm clothing.*

*Most of what I can do I can do without him. I can voice my
opinions and ideas without having abuse bawled at me. I can enjoy
going where I please, when I please, and speak to whoever I like. I
don't have to ask permission to brush my teeth. I am free, there's no
one here kicking me into shape to fit his mould. I was independent
before I met him and now I'm at liberty to be myself again.*

These three women made new lives for themselves. Although it
was a tough struggle they succeeded with courage and
determination. This book has shown you that you, too, can
survive a destructive relationship. Although it will take a
monumental effort, both physically and emotionally, to regain
control over your life, it is worth it.

Remember that:
- You do not have to be subject to your partner's abuse –
  assault is against the law.
- You are not to blame for the abuse you have suffered.
- You need not be ashamed of the past.
- You do not have to be a slave to his needs and demands.
- You do not have to accept his opinions, criticisms and
  erratic behaviour.

- You have the right to get help and support from your doctor, the police, social services, women's refuges, citizens advice bureaux and other voluntary agencies.
- You have the right to speak your mind and show your true feelings.
- Your anger can be used positively.
- You have the power to make your own choices.
- You do not have to do things just to please others.
- You will gain fulfilment by accepting yourself as you are and growing to like yourself.
- You are free to enjoy your life and develop your own talents and interests.
- You can provide your children with a secure and loving home, and the example of a confident, capable adult to learn from.

Appendix 1 Sources of help

Most women's refuges rely on voluntary donations to enable them to continue their work. If you would like to make a donation or offer your services as a volunteer, why not get in touch with your local refuge.

It is often difficult to know where to turn for help, advice and information. This appendix lists the main organisations which offer help to abused women, and tells you how to contact them.

In an emergency

Telephone:
- the police
- your family doctor
- the Samaritans (listed in the phone book under 'Samaritans')
- your nearest refuge (see section below for how to contact a refuge)
- Social services (listed under the name of your local authority in the phone book; outside office hours you can be put in touch with the social worker on emergency duty)

or go to
- your local police station
- the outpatients (casualty) department of your nearest hospital
- your nearest refuge
- the home of a friend, neighbour or religious leader you can trust

Refuges – how to find one

There are three main types of refuge: those belonging to the Women's Aid Federation, independent refuges, and local authority refuges. In an emergency, you will probably want to go to the nearest available refuge, and it may not, at first, matter very much what the refuge is like. In the longer term, or if you leave home after much careful thought and planning, you may wish to go to a refuge where the women staying there, and the refuge workers, share your own particular views or come from the same cultural or ethnic background.

You can obtain the number of your nearest refuge from:
- directory enquiries
- citizens advice bureaux
- Social services
- the Samaritans
- public libraries (ask at the Reference section)
- the police
- your local housing advice centre
- your local law centre
- your local council for voluntary service (listed in the phone book)

In addition, the headquarters of the National Women's Aid Federation (and their regional offices in Wales, Scotland and Northern Ireland) will be able to put you in touch with the nearest refuge belonging to their federation:

National Women's Aid Federation England Ltd
PO Box 391, Bristol BS99 7WS Telephone 0272-420611
Welsh Women's Aid
38-48 Crwys Road, Cardiff, Wales CF2 4NN Telephone 0222-390874
Scottish Women's Aid
11 St Colme Street, Edinburgh, Scotland EH3 6AG Telephone 031-225 8011
Northern Ireland Women's Aid Federation
143a University Street, Belfast, Northern Ireland BT7 1HP Telephone 0232-249041/249358

There is no co-ordinating body linking the many independent refuges that exist throughout the country. However, Chiswick Family Rescue maintains an up-to-date list of independent refuges, and can put callers in touch with a refuge near them. It can also give you the number of your nearest Women's Aid or local authority refuge. The Chiswick refuge accepts women from any part of the UK:
Chiswick Family Rescue
PO Box 855, London W4 4JF Telephone 01-994 4430 (24 hour crisis line)/01-747 0133 (office hours – for general office queries only, e.g. publicity)

Your local social services department will be able to tell you about any refuges they run.

Ethnic minority women

The London and regional offices of the Women's Aid Federation, and Chiswick Family Rescue (addresses and phone numbers above) will be able to put you in touch with refuges specially run by ethnic minority women for abused women of similar backgrounds.

All refuges charge accommodation fees to the women who stay in them, but *do not* let your lack of money stop you going to a refuge in an emergency. The women at the refuge, and the refuge workers, will help you claim welfare benefits and will put you in touch with solicitors who can help you seek maintenance from your husband.

How to get advice about your rights

Under the law, you have rights to live in safety, to be housed if you are homeless, to receive medical treatment and a basic income, if you are without work, to support you and your children. Sometimes it is not easy to discover just what your rights are, or to find out how to claim them. Several organisations, some run by the State, some voluntary, exist to help you. They can offer detailed information and advice, or just someone to share your worries and talk to.

Claiming your rights can be a complicated business, even with help from the experts, so do not feel discouraged or demoralised if, at times, you seem to be making slow progress. It is often a good idea to take a friend along with you when you go to ask advice, make a claim, or see a solicitor. They can give you moral support, and help you to remember all the advice you have been given. It is also a good idea to jot down any questions you may want to ask the experts before you go to see them. In that way, you will be sure of remembering them. Sometimes it is very easy to forget important questions you wanted to ask, only to remember them hours after leaving the meeting with the expert!

The following organisations will help you find out what your rights are, and how to go about claiming them:

Citizens advice bureaux

There is a bureau in most large towns, and sometimes branches or phone links in smaller towns or rural areas. Look them up in the phone book, or, if you have any trouble in finding a branch near you, contact their national headquarters for the address of the nearest bureau. Citizens advice bureaux provide a free, confidential and expert advice service for anyone in need. They can also explain how the legal aid system operates, and can put you in touch with a solicitor who is prepared to undertake legal aid work.

National Association of Citizens Advice Bureaux
115-123 Pentonville Road, London N1 9LZ Telephone 01-833 2181

Housing advice centres

Many large towns have housing advice centres, usually funded by the local council (although some are run by voluntary organisations). These centres exist to help people who have housing problems. To find the centre nearest to you, ask at your local library, at your town hall, or look in the phone book. Their advice is free. Shelter, the national voluntary organisation concerned with homelessness, may be able to give you details of any housing advice services in your area:

Shelter – National Campaign for the Homeless
157 Waterloo Road, London SE1 8XF Telephone 01-633 9377

SHAC is another voluntary organisation which can offer advice on housing in the Greater London area:

SHAC (The London Housing Aid Centre)
189a Old Brompton Road, London SW5 0AR Telephone 01-373 7276/7841

Law centres or legal advice centres

These have been set up in a number of towns to offer free legal advice to people with problems. They will also explain how to apply for legal aid, and can put you in touch with a solicitor who specialises in welfare or family law. If there is one near you, it will be listed in your local phone book. Otherwise you can get the address and phone number of your nearest legal advice centre from:

Law Centres Federation .
Duchess House, 18–19 Warren Street, London W1P 5DB Telephone 01-387 8570

If you have been injured, a law centre, your solicitor or a citizens advice bureau can also help you make an application for compensation to the Criminal Injuries Compensation Board. You can contact the CICB direct to ask for an application form:

Criminal Injuries Compensation Board
Whittington House, 19 Alfred Place, London WC1E 7LG
Telephone 01-636 9501

Department of Health and Social Security (DHSS)

The DHSS publishes a large number of leaflets explaining how
state welfare benefits are calculated. You can obtain copies of
these from Post Offices, or consult them at your local library.
You can make an appointment to discuss your claim for benefits
with one of their officers. Unfortunately these officers are
usually working under great pressure, and so it may take some
time before your case can be discussed. If you feel that your
claim has not received a fair hearing, consult the citizens advice
bureau, your social worker (if you have one) or contact the
Claimants' Union. This is a voluntary organisation which aims
to offer advice to anyone receiving state welfare benefits. To
find out whether there is a branch near you, ask their
headquarters:
National Federation of Claimants Unions
296 Bethnal Green Road, London E2 0AG Telephone 01-739 4173

Social services

You can contact your local social services department to ask to
discuss your problems with a social worker if you are living in
fear of a violent or otherwise abusive partner, if you are worried
about your children, or if you are frightened of losing your
home. The professional social worker who handles your case
will be able to help you make a claim for re-housing, or for
DHSS welfare benefits, and may be able to put you or your
partner in touch with skilled professional help. Ask the
receptionist at your local social services offices (listed under the
name of your local council in the phone book) for an
appointment with a social worker.

Other advice services

In many towns there are advice centres, often organised on
'drop-in' lines, run by a variety of organisations. Some will
cater for the whole population, others will be designed to help
particular groups, for example women, children, or ethnic
minorities. To find out about what advice services exist in your
area, ask
• your local citizens advice bureau
• your local advice centre
• your local law centre
All the above are listed in the phone book.

How to get advice and help with particular problems

You can always ask your family doctor, health visitor or social worker for advice on health or welfare problems. In addition, there are a number of voluntary associations that have been set up to help people with particular problems. Many of these organisations are run on a self-help basis; that is, people facing similar problems have joined together to help themselves and others. Many of these voluntary organisations have local branches; contact their headquarters to find out whether there is a branch near you. You may find that just meeting other people who have been in a similar situation to your own is helpful. Some organisations also have limited funds from which they can make grants or loans; others offer specialised information and advice.

The following national voluntary organisations will also be able to give you information about other voluntary groups that exist to help abused women and their children – and anyone else with problems. Contact the Information Officer in each case:

National Council for Voluntary Organisations
26 Bedford Square, London WC1B 3HU Telephone 01-636 4066
Wales Council for Voluntary Action
Llys Ifor, Heol Crescent, Caerffili, Canol Morgannwyg, Wales CF8 1KL Telephone 0222-869 2224/5/6
Scottish Council for Voluntary Organisations
18–19 Claremont Crescent, Edinburgh, Scotland EH7 4HX Telephone 031-556 3882
Northern Ireland Council for Voluntary Action
2 Annandale Road, Belfast, Northern Ireland BT7 3JH Telephone 0232-640011

Ethnic minority organisations

National Ethnic Minority Advisory Council
2nd and 3rd Floors, 13 Macclesfield Street, London W1V 7HL Telephone 01-349 8765
National Federation of Self-Help Organisations
150 Townmead Road, London SW6 2RA Telephone 01-731 4438/9

Three directories have been published recently which together list over 2,000 voluntary organisations. They should be available in many public libraries or in bookshops:
Voluntary Agencies: The 1988 Directory (Bedford Square Press, 1987)

Health Help '87/88, compiled for Thames Television's HELP!
Programme (Bedford Square Press, 1987)
Springboard '87 (Springboard Publishing Ltd, 1987), a directory
of women's businesses, organisations and community services
in the London area.

For Scotland consult:
Directory of National Voluntary Organisations for Scotland
(Scottish Council for Voluntary Organisations, 1987)

For Northern Ireland consult:
Directory of Voluntary Organisations in Northern Ireland
(Northern Ireland Council for Voluntary Action, 1986)

Parents

Family Holiday Association
Hertford Lodge, East End Road, Finchley, London N3 3QE.
Telephone 01-349 4044
Provides grants to give holidays to parents and children in
need.
Family Rights Group
6–9 Manor Gardens, Holloway Road, London N7 6LA.
Telephone 01-263 4016/9724. Advice line: 01-272 7308 (Mon,
Wed, Fri 9.30–12.30)
Family Service Units
207 Old Marylebone Road, London NW1 5QP Telephone 01-402
5175
Runs groups for children and communities under stress; offers
a welfare rights advice service.
Gingerbread
35 Wellington Street, London WC2E 7BN Telephone 01-240 0953
A self-help group for single parents.
Mothers Apart from their Children
c/o BM Problems, London WC1 3XX
Offers help and advice to mothers living apart from their
children.
National Council for One-Parent Families
255 Kentish Town Road, London NW5 2LX Telephone 01-267
1361
Comprehensive advice services for one-parent families.
Organisation for Parents Under Stress (OPUS)
106 Godstone Road, Whyteleafe, Surrey CR3 06B Telephone
01-645 0469
Aims to prevent child abuse; offers advice and support to
families under stress.

Parent Network
44–46 Caversham Road, London NW5 2DS Telephone 01-485 8535
Runs support groups to help families where there are problems between parents and children.
Parents Anonymous
6–7 Manor Gardens, London N7 6LA Telephone 01-236 8918 (24 hour answering service)
Aims to prevent child abuse; offers confidential help to parents under stress.
Single Parent Links and Special Holidays (SPLASH)
19 North Street, Plymouth, Devon PL4 9AH Telephone 0752-674067
Arranges low-cost holidays for single parents with children.
Working Mothers Association
23 Webbs Road, London SW11 6RU Telephone 01-228 3757
Provides information and advice on childcare for working mothers.

Children

Child Poverty Action Group
21 Macklin Street, London WC2 5HN Telephone 01-242 3225/9194
Provides information on child welfare benefits.
Childline
Telephone 0 800 1111 (freephone, for children in distress)
Children's Legal Centre
20 Compton Terrace, London N1 2UN Telephone 01-359 6251
Runs free advice and information service.
Children's Society
Edward Rudolf House, Margery Street, London WC1X 0JL Telephone 01-387 4299
Runs a variety of childcare services, including children's homes, fostering, social work.
Incest Crisis Line
PO Box 32, Northolt, Middx UB5 4JF Telephone 01-422 5100
Incest Helpline (Wales)
PO Box 350, Cardiff, Wales CF1 3XR Telephone 0222-733929
Incest and Child Sexual Abuse Self-Help Group for Women
c/o The Family Centre, 1 East Albert Road, Kirkcaldy, Fife Telephone 0592 264747 ext 4
Incest and Sexual Abuse – Refuge for Victims
Telephone Belfast (0232) 666049
Kidscape
82 Brook Street, London SW1X 8NF Telephone 01-235 2884

Provides advice and information. Aims to prevent child sexual abuse.

National Childcare Campaign
Wesley House, 4 Wild Court, London WC2B 5AU Telephone 01-405 5617
Offers advice and support to local groups trying to improve local childcare facilities.

National Children's Centre
The Brian Jackson Centre, New North Parade, Huddersfield, West Yorkshire HD1 5JP
Offers advice, information and support for parents and children.

National Children's Home
85 Highbury Park, London N5 1UD Telephone 01-226 2033
For Scotland, dial 100 and ask for Freephone Family Network. Runs a variety of childcare services, including daycare and family advice centres.

National Society for the Prevention of Cruelty to Children
67 Saffron Hill, London EC1N 8RS Telephone 01-242 1626
Offers support, advice and help to children and their families.

Marriage guidance

Catholic Marriage Advisory Council
Clitherow House, 15 Landsowne Road, London W11 3AJ Telephone 01-727 0141

Jewish Marriage Council
23 Ravenshurst Avenue, London NW4 4EL Telephone 01-203 6311

National Council for the Divorced and Separated
13 High Street, Little Shelford, Cambridgeshire CB2 5ES Telephone 0206 396206

National Marriage Guidance Council (RELATE)
Herbert Grey College, Little Church Street, Rugby, Warwickshire CV21 3AP Telephone 0788 73241

Housing

CHAR (Campaign for the Homeless and Rootless)
5–15 Cromer Street, London WC1H 8LS Telephone 01-833 2071
Information on housing matters.

Homeless Action and Accommodation Ltd
52–54 Featherstone Street, London EC1Y 8RT Telephone 01-251 6783
Information and advice for homeless women.

Homes for Homeless People
4th Floor, Smithfield House, Digbeth, Birmingham B5 6BS
Local groups run emergency and longer-term housing schemes,
and day centres.

Housing Debtline
The Birmingham Settlement, 318 Summer Lane, Birmingham
B19 3RL
Telephone 021-359 8501/2/3/4
Telephone advice line for people in legal or financial difficulties
with rents or mortgages.

See also SHAC and Shelter (addresses on page 86).

Drugs, alcohol and related problems

Accept Services UK
Accept Clinic, 200 Seagrave Road, London SW6 1RQ Telephone
01-381 3155
Runs counselling services and clinics for people with alcohol,
tranquilliser or drug problems.

Al-Anon Family Groups
61 Great Dover Street, London SE1 4YF Telephone 01-403 0888
To help families of alcoholics.

Alcohol Concern
305 Grays Inn Road, London WC1X 8QF Telephone 01-833 3471
Helps to set up new services to help alcoholics; provides
information.

Alcoholics Anonymous
PO Box 1, Stonebow House, Stonebow, York YO1 2NJ
Telephone 0904-644026/01-352 3001
A self-help group for alcoholics

Drugline
9a Brockley Cross, London SE4 2AB Telephone 01-692 4975
Telephone advice and counselling for people with drug
problems.

Families Anonymous
5–7 Parsons Green, London SW6 4UL Telephone 01-731 8060
Helps families of drug abusers.

Gamblers Anonymous and Gam-Anon
17–23 Blantyre Street, Cheyne Walk, London SW10 0DT
Telephone 01-352 3060
Self-help group for people with gambling problems. Gam-Anon
helps families.

Life Without Tranquillisers
Lynmouth, Devon EX35 6EE
Provides information and advice to people with problems
caused by tranquillisers or sleeping tablets.

Release
c/o 347a Upper Street, London N1 0PD Telephone 01-289 1123
(24-hour emergency number 01-603 8654)
Gives advice on drugs and legal problems.

Re-Solv
St Mary's Chambers, 1 Station Road, Stone, Staffs ST15 8JP
Telephone 0785-817885/46097
Advice and information on solvent abuse.

Tranx (UK) Ltd
25a Masons Avenue, Wealdstone, Harrow, Middx HA3 5AH
Advice, information and support for people with problems
caused by tranquillisers.

Women's Alcohol Centre
254 St Pauls Road, Islington, London N1 2LJ Telephone 01-226
4581
Counselling, advice and information for women about alcohol
abuse.

How to contact a women's group or find out about assertiveness courses

---

You might find it helpful to discuss your own experiences as an
abused woman with other women, or you may simply be
interested in meeting and making friends with other women, or
in exploring ways of living as a single woman now that you.
have left your male partner. In many towns, women's groups
meet regularly. Some are purely social, others may be based on
shared political, religious or cultural beliefs. Others are more
like evening classes, and encourage women to learn new skills,
or to rebuild their shattered self-confidence. Assertiveness
training is designed to help women take control of their lives,
and to stand up for themselves and their children in a positive,
but not aggressive way. There are also many national women's
organisations with branches throughout the country. These
welcome new members, and are a good way of meeting new
friends with similar interests.
To find out about these organisations, contact:

Women's groups and courses for women

Many women's groups are local, and information about them is
spread by word of mouth, or on noticeboards. WIRES tries to
keep a register of local groups:
Women's Information Referral and Enquiry Service (WIRES)
PO Box 20, Oxford, Oxon Telephone 0865 240991

Feminist Library and Information Centre
Hungerford House, Victoria Embankment, London WC2N 6PA
Telephone 01-930 0715 (for information about Women's Studies courses)
Your local college of further or higher education, or the adult education department of your local authority will have information about courses designed specially for women. Often, these courses are free, or half-price, to women claiming welfare benefits. Other adult education courses are run by organisations like the Workers Educational Association, by various university Extra-Mural Boards, and by the Open University. Your local library should be able to give you information about these, otherwise contact:
Workers Educational Association
Temple House, 9 Upper Berkley Street, London WIH 8BY 01-402 5608/9
The Open University
Walton Hall, Milton Keynes, MK7 6AA Telephone 0908-74066

National women's organisations

These are just some of the many nationally-based women's organisations:
Catholic Women's League
48 Great Peter Street, London SW1P 2HA Telephone 01-222 2495
Co-operative Women's Guild
342 Hoe Street, Walthamstow, London E17 9PX Telephone 01-520 4902
King's Cross Women's Centre
71 Tonbridge Street, London WC1H 9DZ Telephone 01-837 7509 (will answer enquiries from outside London)
League of Jewish Women
Woburn House, Upper Woburn Place, London WC1H 0EP Telephone 01-387 7688
National Association of Women's Clubs
5 Vernon Rise, King's Cross Road, London WC1X 9EP Telephone 01-837 1434
National Federation of Women's Institutes
39 Eccleston Street, London SW1 9NT Telephone 01-730 7212
National Free Church Women's Council
27 Tavistock Sqaure, London WC1H 9HH Telephone 01-387 8413
National Union of Townswomens Guilds
Chamber of Commerce House, 75 Harborne Road, Birmingham B15 3DA 021-455 6868

National Women's Register
245 Warwick Road, Solihull, West Midlands B92 7AH
Telephone 021-706 1101
Rights of Women
52–54 Featherstone Street, London EC1Y 8RT Telephone 01-251 6577

Ethnic minority women

The following national organisations may be able to tell you whether there is a women's group affiliated to them in your area:
Bangladeshi Women's Organisation
91 Highbury Hills, London N5 1SX Telephone 01-359 5836
Camden Chinese Community Centre
173 Arlington Road, London NW1 7EY Telephone 01-267 3019
Carribbean House Group and Westindian Concern Ltd
Caribbean House, Bridport Place, London N1 5DS Telephone 01-729 0986
Chinese Information and Advice Centre
152–156 Shaftesbury Avenue, London WC2 Telephone 01-836 8291
Confederation of Indian Organisations UK
11 North Avenue, Harrow, Middx HA2 7AE Telephone 01-928 9889/836 9089
Federation of Spanish Associations in the UK
116 Ladbroke Grove, London W1 5NE Telephone 01-221 2007
India Welfare Society
11 Middle Row, London W10 5AT Telephone 01-969 9493
Indian Workers Association
Southall Town Hall, High Street, Southall, Middx UB1 3HA Telephone 01-574 6019
Joint Council for the Welfare of Immigrants
115 Old Street, London EC1V 9JR Telephone 01-251 8706
Kala Ujamaa Ltd
Southbank House, Black Prince Road, London SE1 7SJ Telephone 01-582 9116/587 0243
Latin American Women's Rights Service
Beauchamp Lodge, 2 Warwick Crescent, London W6 6NO Telephone 01-289 1601
National Federation of Cypriots in Great Britain
4 Porchester Terrace, London W2 3TL Telephone 01-723 4001/402 8904
Pakistan Welfare Organisation
181 Haydens Road, London SW19 8TS Telephone 01-542 6176

Southall Black Sisters
52 Norwood Road, Southall Middx UB2 4DW Telephone 01-571 9595
Standing Conference of West Indian Organisations
5 Westminster Bridge Road, London SE1 7WX Telephone 01-928 7861/2
Union of Turkish Women in Great Britain
110 Clarence Road, London E5 Telephone 01-986 1358/1405
West Indian Women's Association
71 Pound Lane, Willesdon, London NW10 2HU Telephone 01-541 4827

The national organisations listed on page 88 may also be able to pass on information about ethnic minority women's associations.

How to find a therapist or counsellor

Counselling and psychotherapy are provided free under the National Health Service, free (or for a very small charge) by some refuges, rape crisis centres and voluntary organisations, and on a fee-paying basis by 'private' counsellors and therapists. All counsellors and therapists will treat everything you say in the strictest confidence.

Free or very low-cost counselling and therapy

National Health Service
Ask your family doctor, health visitor, social worker, or family planning clinic if they can refer you to a therapist or counsellor under the National Health Service (NHS). The NHS employs many highly-trained professionals in specialist psychiatric hospitals or out-patient departments. Unfortunately, the demand for their services is very great, and much of their time is spent treating people with serious acute or chronic mental illness once they have been admitted to, or recently discharged from, hospital. However, some counselling or therapy is available on the NHS, and it is well worth while asking about it. If you feel that your request for NHS treatment has not received a fair hearing, or if you would like to know more about the range of psychiatric services available under the NHS, then the voluntary organisation 'MIND' might be able to help you. Contact their national headquarters for the address of your local branch:
MIND (National Association for Mental Health)
22 Harley Street, London W1N 2ED Telephone 01-637 0741

Refuges and rape crisis centres
Professional therapists and counsellors are also employed by some refuges and rape crisis centres to give free advice to abused women. Other refuges may offer free counselling by carefully-trained volunteers; many of these women may themselves have suffered abuse, or faced other serious problems, at some time in the past. Now they want to offer what they have learned from their own experiences to help others. Contact your nearest refuge (see page 84) for how to do this) or your nearest rape crisis centre (ask directory enquiries) to find out what free counselling services they can offer at the refuge or rape crisis centre. Some refuges, social work departments, hospital out-patients departments and voluntary organisations also run therapy groups, where women can meet and discuss their problems together in an atmosphere of trust and mutual support. Sometimes a counsellor or therapist is on hand to offer advice or to comment if requested. Ask your doctor, your social worker or your local refuge if any groups like this exist in your area.

Voluntary organisations
Your doctor, social worker or local refuge may also be able to tell you about any counselling schemes run by voluntary organisations in your area. Like refuges, voluntary organisations may employ professional therapists or counsellors, or may rely on trained volunteers. Since many voluntary organisations are short of funds, a small fee is sometimes charged, although counselling will usually be free to women on low incomes. The marriage guidance voluntary organisations listed on page 91 will also know of free counselling services in your area (many of them offer counselling as part of their own activities), and many of the organisations listed on pages 88–93 will also be able to offer some sort of counselling to people facing specific problems. If you are under 25, you might also like to contact your nearest Brook Advisory Centre; you can get its address from:
Brook Advisory Centres
153a East Street, London SE17 2SD Telephone 01-708 1234/1390.
Brook Centres specialise in helping young people with advice on sexual and relationship problems.

Private (fee-paying) therapy and counselling

Professional therapists sometimes work privately as individuals, or join together to set up therapy or counselling centres, and offer their services to fee-paying clients. Many private therapists or counsellors are prepared to reduce their fees to people on low incomes, but you cannot expect them to give their services for free – after all, they have a living to earn! Many abused women (and many men and women with other problems) will be unable to afford private counselling or therapy, but even for those who can afford the fees, it can often be difficult to know which therapist or counsellor to turn to. You can start by asking your doctor, your colleagues or your friends if they can recommend anyone, or you can contact one of the organisations listed below.

The following voluntary organisations should be able to suggest the names and addresses of private counsellors or therapists in your area. Two of them, the Women's Therapy Centre and the Westminster Pastoral Foundation, also offer low-cost therapy/counselling to people on low incomes.

British Association for Counselling
37a Sheep Street, Rugby, Warwickshire CV21 3BX Telephone 0788 78328/9
British Association of Psychotherapists
121 Hendon Lane, London N3 3PR Telephone 01-346 1747
Westminster Pastoral Foundation
23 Kensington Square, London W8 5HN Telephone 01-937 6956
Women's Therapy Centre
6 Manor Gardens, London N7 6LA Telephone 01-263 6200

Appendix 2 Useful publications

Binney, Val, Harkell, Gina & Nixon, Judy. *Leaving Violent Men: A Study of Refuges and Housing for Battered Women*, Women's Aid Federation England, 1981

Carew-Jones, Melanie & Watson, Hester. *Making the Break: A practical, sympathetic and encouraging guide for women experiencing violence in their lives*, Penguin Books, 1985

McNicholas, Anne. *Going it Alone: Your Rights and Relationship Breakdown. A Guide for Unmarried Women*, SHAC, 1986

Mitchell, Ann. *Coping with Separation and Divorce*, Chambers, 1986

Nicarthy, Ginny. *Getting Free: A Handbook for Women in Abusive Relationships*, Washington: Seal Press, 1982

Pizzey, Erin. *Scream Quietly or the Neighbours Will Hear*, Penguin 1974, reprinted 1979. (Out of print but probably available in most public libraries.)

Taylor, Liz McNeill. *Bringing Up Children On Your Own*, Fontana, 1985

Witherspoon, Sue. *A Woman's Place: Your Rights and Relationship Beakdown. A Guide for Married Women*, SHAC, 1985

Appendix 3 Acts which provide protection for abused women in England and Wales

The information below summarises the Acts which will provide protection for abused women. It looks complicated, but don't let that deter you from seeking legal advice to try and secure a safe and peaceful life for you and for your children. You will need a solicitor's expert advice if you plan to take any of the proceedings listed below.

Domestic Violence and Matrimonial Proceedings Act 1976

Who may apply?

Married or unmarried women. The only unmarried women who can apply are those who are living with their partner when the violence/bad behaviour occurred or those who were living with their partner when the troubles began, which may have continued after the separation.

You can apply

If your partner is molesting, harassing or being violent towards you.

Orders granted

The court can:
- order your partner not to molest you or your child
- order that he not get anyone else to do this on his behalf
- exclude your partner from your home or from a specified area around your home (violence does not have to be proved to get your partner excluded from your home)

* order your partner to let you back into and remain in your house

Which court?

County Court. The public will not be allowed into the court.

Power of arrest

May be included if:
* your partner has caused actual harm to you or your children and
* he is likely to do so again. Even though an injunction has been asked for, if a man promises not to be violent again judges often will not always attach a power of arrest

If the court accepts an undertaking from your partner not to assault you again and no injunction is made, then a power of arrest cannot be attached.

Domestic Proceedings and Magistrates Courts Act 1978

Who may apply?

Married women only.

You can apply

if there has been physical violence or threats of physical violence.

Orders granted

The court can:
* make a personal protection order telling your partner not to use or threaten to use violence against you or your child
* order that he not get anyone else to do it on his behalf
* grant an expedited personal protection order (for example in cases of extreme danger), but there is no power to exclude a man from the home on such an expedited order
* issue an exclusion order (similar to an 'ouster' order from the county court) if the magistrates are satisfied that you or your children are in danger of being physically injured by your partner and that he has either used violence or threatened to use violence in the past
* make orders concerning financial provision and children

Which court?

Magistrates.

Power of arrest

May be included if physical violence has been used in the past and is likely to be used again. However, magistrates may not do this if your husband promises not to assault you again.

The Matrimonial Homes Act 1983 and within divorce proceedings

Who may apply?

Married women with custody of children who are being harassed.

Orders granted

The court can:
- order your husband not to molest you or your children (as part of divorce/judicial separations/nullity proceedings; such an order is probably not available after Decree Absolute except concerning children, and the order may include the woman if she has custody)
- order that he not get anyone else to molest you or your children on his behalf
- issue an ouster order which means he will have to leave your home and not come within a specified area around the home (the order can only be granted where no petition has been filed or within the divorce suit if the petition has been filed. Ousters are not available after Decree Absolute, except possibly where children are involved as above)
- order your husband to let you back into and remain in your house
- issue an ex parte injunction in an emergency

Which court?

County Court (occasionally High Court).

Power of arrest

May be included if:
- your partner has caused actual harm to you or your children
- he is likely to do so again. Even though an injunction has

been asked for, if a man promises not to be violent again judges often will not always include a power of arrest

The Guardianship of Minors Act 1971 and 1973 and wardship proceedings

Who may apply?

Married or unmarried women. The Guardianship of Minors Act is mainly concerned with the welfare of children. Under this Act you can apply for custody, access and maintenance, provided you are not living with your partner. For example, you may wish to apply for custody of your children urgently if you have had to leave them behind in order to escape your partner. It is also possible to get injunctions and ouster orders under this Act, although ouster orders are usually only granted in very limited circumstances.

If you are worried that your partner will kidnap the children or take them out of the country without your permission he can be prevented from doing so either under the Guardianship of Minors Act or wardship proceedings.

You can apply

At any time, either where the partners are not married or before divorce or judicial separation proceedings, during such proceedings (although that is unusual) but importantly, also after Decree Absolute.

Orders granted

Custody, non-molestation and ouster injunctions can be granted under the Guardianship of Minors Act. The court can also make orders for maintenance of children and access. If the tenancy is in your name or you own the house an ouster can be granted. The court has *not* the power to grant an ouster where it is the man's tenancy or he owns the property, or you are joint tenants or joint owners.

Under wardship proceedings your child can be made a ward of court. This means the court is officially in charge of what happens to the child. The court must be consulted about major decisions in the child's life. Normally the child is allowed to live with you, but sometimes the court will place the child in the care of social services who then take responsibility. The court has the power to order the man not to take the children out of the country. It can grant an injunction to prevent him from assaulting you or the children. It can also decide on other matters such as custody, access and maintenance.

Which court?

- Guardianship of Minors Act in the High Court, County Court or Magistrates Court
- Wardship proceedings in the High Court only

Power of arrest

No power of arrest.

Civil action in tort for assault/battery, nuisance or trespass

Who may apply?

Married or unmarried women. Unmarried women who do not live with their partners as husband, wife, or women who make an application after a Decree Absolute may find this relief particularly useful. Homosexual couples can also apply.

You can apply

If you have been assaulted, harassed or there has been a trespass.

Orders granted:

- a non-molestation injunction relating to the woman and/or the children
- an order to prevent your partner coming to your own property
- damages (if quantifiable damage has been suffered by the woman by way of physical injury or damage to property, this relief can be useful!)
- Ex parte injunctions
- Power of arrest

Which court?

County Court or High Court.

References

1 Andrews, Bernice. 'Violence in Normal Homes', paper delivered at Marriage Research Centre Conference on Family Violence, 15 April 1987.

2 Green, Paul (Chairman). (Unpublished) 'Metropolitan Police Working Party Report into Domestic Violence', January 1986.

3 London Strategic Policy Unit, Police Monitoring and Research Group Briefing Paper No. 1, *Police Response to Domestic Violence*, 1986.

4 Jaffé, Peter and Burroes, Carole Anne. *An Integrated Response to Wife Assault: A Community Approach Model*, Ottawa, the Solicitor-General of Canada, 1982.

5 Edwards, Susan. 'Police Attitudes and Disposition in Domestic Disputes: The London Study', *Police Journal*, vol LVIX(3), July/September 1986, pp 230–241.

6 Roy, Maria (ed). *The Abusive Partner*, New York: Van Nostrand Reinhold, 1980.

7 Dobash, Russell and Dobash, Rebecca. *Violence Against Wives*, New York: Free Press, 1979.

8 Jaffé, Peter. 'A Research Study to Evaluate the Impact and Effectiveness of the Policy Directive that Police Lay Charges in All Domestic Violence Incidents where Reasonable and Probable Grounds Exist', London, Ontario: London Family Court Clinic and Department of Psychology, University of Western Ontario, 1985.

References

Index